HANDBOOK OF HYPNOTIC TECHNIQUES, VOL. 1:

FAVORITE METHODS OF MASTER CLINICIANS

EDITED BY MARK P. JENSEN, PHD

Denny
Creek
Press

Handbook of Hypnotic Techniques, Vol. 1: Favorite Methods of Master Clinicians
Edition: 1st Edition
Book 4 in the *Voices of Experience*® series.
Editor: Mark P. Jensen

ISBN# paperback: 978-1-946832-12-2
ISBN# Kindle: 978-1-946832-13-9

Library of Congress # (paperback edition only): 2019906818

Published by:
Denny Creek Press
Kirkland, Washington
dennycreekpress@yahoo.com

Denny
Creek
Press

Cover art by Liza Brown of Modern Art Media
Interior design by Elizabeth Beeton of B10 Mediaworx

Library of Congress Cataloging-in-Publication Data

    Handbook of Hypnotic Techniques, Vol. 1: Favorite Methods of Master Clinicians / Mark P. Jensen, editor.

    Includes bibliographic references
    ISBN 978-1-946832-12-2 (alk. paper)
    1. Hypnotism—Therapeutic Use 2. Psychotherapy

Dedicated with love to my wonderful siblings:
Ann, Luhr, Carol,
Joan, and Eric

Praise for
Handbook of Hypnotic Techniques, Vol. 1

"A fascinating, enriching, and practical book that illustrates the many complex roads that lead to the heart of Hypnotic Therapy. The authors, who are expert drivers of these roads, teach us how to drive safely, avoid potential pitfalls, and effectively achieve therapeutic goals that are respectful of each client's nature." —Camillo Loriedo, MD, PhD, Co-editor of *TranceForming Ericksonian Methods*, and Past-President, International Society of Hypnosis

"Like a road sign, good clinical technique points to something beyond itself—to the core competencies of an effective therapist. In this book, a team of master clinicians describe and then beautifully illustrate essential skills for engaging the mind's hidden resources and growth potential." —Dan Short, PhD, lead author of *Hope and Resiliency: Understanding the Psychotherapeutic Strategies of Milton H. Erickson*, in co-authorship with Betty Alice Erickson and Roxanna Erickson Klein

"This is a wonderful compilation of innovative clinical techniques for hypnosis practice. The book includes chapters by 11 respected clinicians from all over the world, allowing for a blend of mastering techniques, and developing one's own voice and style individualized for each patient's needs. I highly recommend this beautiful addition to the *Voices of Experience*® series." —Donald Moss, PhD, Dean, College of Integrative Medicine and Health Sciences, Saybrook University, and President of the Society for Clinical & Experimental Hypnosis

"This latest entry into the superb *Voices of Experience*® series features an exceptionally talented group of internationally known clinicians who each generously share their favorite hypnotic techniques. It's easy to see why these techniques are regarded as favorites: They feature skillful combinations of creativity and purposefulness, structure and flexibility, and timeliness and timelessness. Clinicians who hope to learn solid, practical approaches to the use of hypnosis from recognized experts will undoubtedly appreciate this wonderful volume." —Michael D. Yapko, PhD, clinical psychologist and author of *Trancework: An Introduction to the Practice of Clinical Hypnosis* (5th edition) and *Taking Hypnosis to the Next Level: Valuable Tips for Enhancing Your Clinical Practice*

About the *Voices of Experience®* series

Research demonstrates that experienced hypnosis practitioners obtain better outcomes than hypnosis practitioners who are relatively new to the field. For example, Barabasz and colleagues found that the participants in a study of smoking cessation who were treated by clinicians experienced in the use of hypnosis evidenced over *four times* greater treatment response than participants who were treated by clinical psychology interns with minimal training (Barabasz et al., 1986). Although this finding may seem intuitively obvious, clinician experience has *not* been found to play a role in treatment outcome for many other (nonhypnotic) psychological therapies (Berman & Norton, 1985; Durlak, 1979; Shapiro & Shapiro, 1982).

Thus, hypnosis outcomes appear to be particularly sensitive to the benefits of experience. This makes sense, given that hypnosis involves the creative application of specific techniques for enhancing patient readiness to accept new ideas (i.e., the hypnotic induction; Jensen, 2017), as well as the skilled use of language to develop and offer suggestions for changes in how the patient feels, thinks, or behaves. By observing the patient's immediate and longer-term response to treatment, clinicians discover and refine effective techniques and hone their use of language. Through this process they learn what works and what does not work.

Given the widespread use of hypnosis, clinicians in some regions will likely discover and develop techniques that other clinicians may not have (yet) discovered. Thus, there are master clinicians worldwide who are using effective methods that clinicians in other parts of the world may not have heard of or discovered yet.

Unfortunately, while many of the world's most experienced clinicians facilitate workshops in their own countries, they do not always teach at international conferences such as the tri-annual World Congress of Medical and Clinical Hypnosis (www.ishhypnosis.org). Nor is every practicing clinician able to participate in workshops that are offered around world. The purpose of the *Voices of Experience*® series is to give practicing clinicians access to the wealth of knowledge held by master clinicians throughout the world, in order to increase the ease and efficacy of treatment.

To make this information easily accessible, in the chapters contained in the series' books, the authors describe the theory or ideas that underlie their favorite hypnotic approaches and techniques. They also provide a transcript or script that illustrates the technique or approach they find useful, along with commentary. Thus, each chapter is much like having an opportunity to participate in a workshop offered by the authors. I hope and anticipate that readers will enjoy learning, and then incorporating into their practice, the wisdom and experience shared in this series.

Mark P. Jensen
Editor, *Voices of Experience*®

References

Barabasz, A. F., Baer, L., Sheehan, D. V., & Barabasz, M. (1986). A three-year follow-up of hypnosis and restricted environmental stimulation therapy for smoking. *International Journal of Clinical and Experimental Hypnosis, 34*, 169-181.

Berman, J. S., & Norton, N. C. (1985). Does professional training make a therapist more effective? *Psychological Bulletin, 98*, 401-407.

Durlak, J. A. (1979). Comparative effectiveness of paraprofessional and professional helpers. *Psychological Bulletin, 86*, 80-92.

Jensen, M. P. (2017). *The art and practice of hypnotic induction: Favorite methods of master clinicians.* Kirkland, WA: Denny Creek Press.

Shapiro, D. A., & Shapiro, D. (1982). Meta-analysis of comparative therapy outcome studies: A replication and refinement. *Psychological Bulletin, 92*, 581-604.

Also available in the *Voices of Experience®* series...

Book 1. *The Art and Practice of Hypnotic Induction: Favorite Methods of Master Clinicians*

In this volume, 11 master clinicians with over 350 years of combined clinical experience discuss the key factors necessary for effective hypnotic inductions and provide specific examples of the inductions they have found to be most effective.

Praise for *The Art and Practice of Hypnotic Induction*:

"*The Art and Practice of Hypnotic Induction* is a treasure trove of inductions with an exciting variety to accommodate patients' and clinicians' personal styles, to find the right voice." —Elvira V. Lang, MD, FSIR, FSCEH

"This is a rich read. *The Art and Practice of Hypnotic Induction* encompasses hypnotic language, the therapeutic relationship, conceptual and systemic underpinnings—the very fabric of therapy." —Leora Kuttner, PhD

"A fundamental reference for both the tyro and the expert. This entrancing collection is a must read for those interested in contemporary hypnotic practice." —Jeffrey K. Zeig, PhD

Book 2. *Hypnotic Techniques for Chronic Pain Management: Favorite Methods of Master Clinicians*

In this volume, written by and for clinicians, 13 highly experienced physicians, psychologists, and therapists from around the world describe the hypnotic strategies they have found to be most effective for chronic pain management.

Praise for *Hypnotic Techniques for Chronic Pain Management*:

"The contributors to *Hypnotic Techniques for Chronic Pain Management* are well-known pioneers and innovative practitioners from America, Europe, and Asia. The book provides an abundance of ideas for chronic pain treatment, which even very experienced pain specialists will find inspiring and useful." — Bernhard Trenkle, Dipl Psych

"*Hypnotic Techniques for Chronic Pain Management* offers an impressive number of tools for addressing the critical psychological and psychosocial issues underlying chronic pain." — Howard Hall, PhD

"It is truly a pleasure and enlightening to learn from the outstanding master clinicians who contributed to *Hypnotic Techniques for Chronic Pain Management*" — Stefan J. Friedrichsdorf, MD

Book 3. *Hypnosis for Acute and Procedural Pain Management: Favorite Methods of Master Clinicians*

Hypnosis has proven efficacy for reducing the pain associated with acute injuries and medical procedures. In this edited volume, written by and for clinicians, 10 highly experienced physicians, psychologists, and therapists from around the world describe the hypnotic strategies they have found to be most useful and effective for acute pain management.

Praise for *Hypnosis for Acute and Procedural Pain Management*:

"Looking for a way to change minds about clinical hypnosis? *Hypnosis for Acute and Procedural Pain Management* reads like a TED talk, gathering international expert voices into one concise and practical volume. For clinicians, beginners and experienced alike, it provides theoretical fundamentals and a diversity of techniques to communicate the calm, safe, ego-strengthening climate that alters the mind's perception of pain." —Julie H. Linden, PhD

"The outstanding *Hypnosis for Acute and Procedural Pain Management* is a welcome addition to the field—and to my own library. Each chapter is packed with practical advice and specific hypnotic strategies that I can immediately apply to help my patients be more comfortable and empowered." —Elvira Lang, MD, FSIR, FSCEH

CONTRIBUTORS

Consuelo Casula, Lic Psych
Private Practice
Milan, Italy
consuelocasula@gmail.com

George P. Glaser, LCSW, DAHB
Private Practice
Austin, TX, USA
george@georgeglaser.com

Mark P. Jensen, PhD, FASCH
University of Washington
Seattle, WA, USA
mjensen@uw.edu

Stephen R. Lankton, LCSW, DAHB, FASCH
Private Practice
Phoenix, AZ, USA
steve@lankton.com

Julie Linden, PhD
Private Practice
Philadelphia, PA &
Rangeley, ME, USA
julie@drjulielinden.com

Shigeru Matsuki, LCP, Chmn JSCH, FJSH
Hanazono University
and Private Practice
Kyoto, Japan
K6950605@kadai.jp

Guy H. Montgomery, PhD
Center for Behavioral Oncology
Ichan School of Medicine at
Mount Sinai
New York, NY, USA
guy.montgomery@mssm.edu

Michael Schekter, MD
Private Practice
Lausannne, Switzerland
schekter@citycable.ch

Enayatollah Shahidi, MD
Private Practice
Tehran, Iran
dr.enayat.shahidi@gmail.com

Dorothea T. Thomaßen, MD
Private Practice
Frankfurt, Germany
dorothea.thomassen@hotmail.com

Moshe S. Torem, MD
Northeast Ohio Medical University
Rootstown, OH, USA
toremsr@gmail.com

CONTENTS

CHAPTER 1: Introduction ⸺⸺⸺⸺⸺⸺⸺⸺⸺⸺ 1

Mark P. Jensen

CHAPTER 2: Age Progression as a Therapeutic Modality ⸺⸺ 11

Moshe S. Torem

**CHAPTER 3: A Practical Approach to Age
Regression Therapy** ⸺⸺⸺⸺⸺⸺⸺⸺⸺⸺⸺⸺ 29

Michael Schekter

**CHAPTER 4: Ego-Strengthening Tool for the
Empowerment of Women** ⸺⸺⸺⸺⸺⸺⸺⸺⸺⸺ 55

Julie Linden

**CHAPTER 5: Poetic Language and Hypnosis: The
Interplay of Rhythm, Spaces, and Suggestion** ⸺⸺⸺ 67

George Glaser

**CHAPTER 6: Use of Multiple-Embedded Metaphors to
Facilitate Change** ⸺⸺⸺⸺⸺⸺⸺⸺⸺⸺⸺⸺⸺ 82

Stephen R. Lankton

CHAPTER 7: A Common Factors Approach to Hypnosis ⸺⸺ 95

Guy H. Montgomery

**CHAPTER 8: Utilizing, Reframing, and Expanding Patients'
Metaphors** ⸺⸺⸺⸺⸺⸺⸺⸺⸺⸺⸺⸺⸺⸺⸺ 108

Consuelo Casula

**CHAPTER 9: The Hypnotic Trance Space Theory (Matsuki
Method): Clinicians and Patients Working Together
to Build a Therapeutic Trance "Space"** ⸺⸺⸺⸺⸺ 123

Shigeru Matsuki

CHAPTER 10: Using Hypnotic Reflective Listening to Identify Effective Suggestions for Behavior Change 140

Mark P. Jensen

CHAPTER 11: The Door Technique 171

Enayatollah Shahidi

CHAPTER 12: Remembering Well-Being: The U-Assessment and Therapeutic Protocol 186

Dorothea Thomaßen

ABOUT THE EDITOR 211

CHAPTER 1

Introduction

Mark P. Jensen

Hypnotic techniques are the foundation of effective clinical hypnosis. Classic techniques include those for hypnotic induction (e.g., arm levitation, eye roll), specific methods such as the affect bridge (Watkins, 1970), and more general skills, such as Milton Erickson's "utilization" approach (Erickson, 1959) or eliciting a "yes set" to enhance a client's overall response to hypnotic suggestions (Erickson et al., 1976).

Erickson (1985) described very well the importance of being familiar with effective hypnotic techniques when he wrote:

> We feel that it is important for you to know as many different techniques as possible, for the only way you can develop your own technique is by an awareness of all the different techniques—whether it is the house-tree-man technique, the coin technique, the relaxation technique, or whatever it happens to be. ... Therefore you should be acquainted with all the various techniques, and you should want to practice them. (p. 141)

No surgeon should perform a surgery without knowing the most up-to-date and effective surgical techniques.

Maestros spend years learning and perfecting ways to elicit the right sounds from their instruments. Knowledge about hypnotic techniques is no less important to the effective application of clinical hypnosis.

At the same time, a dependence on techniques, especially when or if they are used the same way with every client, can decrease efficacy. It is essential that once learned, clinicians adapt their methods so that they fit the clinician's own style and approach, and then tailor each application of a skill to what the client needs at that particular time. While the best surgeons will be familiar with the both the classic *and* the most up-to-date techniques for a procedure, each patient and surgical situation is unique and will call for different applications. Michael D. Yapko (2018) expressed this idea very well in his book *Taking Hypnosis to the Next Level* when discussing the use of hypnotic scripts:

> Many people practice hypnosis by using prepared scripts published in articles or books. ... Regardless of how good the script might be, though, it is still a script. It inevitably speaks to clients in an impersonal way since the script was not created for that specific individual. (p. 26)

Thus, while on the one hand it is very important to be exposed to, to learn, and then be able to use a variety of techniques and approaches, ultimately all methods should be adapted and tailored to each client and to each therapeutic context.

In this fourth book of the *Voices of Experience*® series, 11 master clinicians describe classic techniques that they have adapted, or hypnotic techniques and approaches that they have invented and developed, all of which they have found to be particularly effective in their clinical practice.

In the first chapter after this Introduction (Chapter 2), Moshe S. Torem describes an age progression approach that he has perfected over many years in his decades of work as a psychiatrist. This technique involves first, identifying a specific outcome goal (e.g., reduced pain, improved mood, behavior change) that is both valued and possible. Then, following a hypnotic induction, patients are invited to experience "mental time-travel" to a time when the goal has been realized. During the session, they can experience themselves as having achieved the goal, along with all of its psychological and physical benefits. Suggestions are made for the patient to internalize the sense of accomplishment and goal achievement both consciously and unconsciously, and to bring this "back" with them to the present. Additional internalization of the experience occurs with debriefing and as the patient writes about the experience after the session. Like all of the other techniques described in this volume, Torem's Back From the Future procedure can be used to address a great variety of psychological, behavioral, and health problems. The method's overall efficacy and adaptability for addressing many, if not most, therapeutic targets argue strongly for its use.

While the technique described by Moshe S. Torem invites patients to travel into their *future*, an age *regression* technique is described in Chapter 3 by Michael Schekter—a highly experienced psychiatrist and psychotherapist. With this approach, the patient is invited to travel into his or her past. The goal of this approach is to replace negative automatic and repetitive emotional and behavioral responses to current problems or difficulties with more resourceful and adaptive ones. Schekter identifies two categories of age regression strategies: (1) a *positive* age regression technique, during which the patient identifies and then nurtures a signature strength or resource that they can use to address a current problem; and (2) a *negative* age regression technique, during which the patient recalls what had been a negative or traumatic event, but this time re-experiences the event while effectively and successfully managing it. With both approaches, the patient brings into their present new or strengthened resources, insights, and/or a sense and "memory" of successful coping. Schekter describes a clear and easy to follow multi-step protocol that facilitates the process of utilizing and nurturing the patient's own strengths and creativity for problem resolution.

Julie H. Linden is well known in the international hypnosis community for her impactful and effective clinical work, her teaching, and her leadership. In Chapter 4, she describes a 5Es model of feminist hypnotherapy that involve Empathy, Ego-strength, Embodiment, Equality, and Empowerment. Linden provides a transcript of a specific technique, the Identity Portraiture technique, that she has found to be useful for helping women discover their identities as women, providing an important step in nurturing their strength and power. Following trance induction, the patient is invited to gather together the people that have influenced her identity as a woman. She is made aware that each of these individuals has a gift to give, and she may choose to accept or not accept that gift. She then assimilates this experience, which includes taking in any contributions to individual strengths that she wishes to nurture. As Linden points out, although the example transcript focuses on ego-strengthening for patients who are women, the technique can easily be adapted to facilitate ego-strengthening in any category or class of individuals associated with cultural identity. For example, categories defined by gender, race or ethnicity, family role (e.g., mother or father), or occupation, among many others.

George P. Glaser is a clinical social worker with over four decades of experience in the clinical applications of hypnosis. In Chapter 5, he notes that the way that hypnotic suggestions are communicated—the rhythm, the accompanying body movements and facial expressions—that is, the *poetry* of the suggestions, influences the overall experience as well as the outcome for his clients. In his chapter, Glaser describes his lyrical approach to making hypnosis more effective. With this approach, he seeks to present the induction and suggestions as poems: metaphoric language that utilizes and incorporates the words and imagery of the client during the hypnotic session. Glaser notes, that in order for this to be successful, it is essential to pay close attention to both the client and to the therapist's own internal responses as the client describes the presenting problem. In particular, it is useful to listen for and then utilize the refrains—repetitive phrases—that may describe the client's sticking points.

In Chapter 6, Stephen R. Lankton, a clinical social worker with decades of clinical, teaching, and writing experience, describes the Multiple Embedded Metaphors technique. In this approach, a number of (often three) therapeutic metaphors are offered to the patient, such that each metaphor or story is interrupted by the next metaphor or story, until a final metaphor is presented, after which each of the embedded stories are systematically finished in turn. Each metaphor potentially addresses different or related therapeutic goals. Often, the last (embedded) metaphor is the one that addresses the most critical (or most threatening) therapeutic goal. The power of this technique to address more forbidding issues, as well as its propensity to address more than one therapeutic goal at a time, are two of its strengths. Its efficacy may be explained by its apparent ability to enhance hypnotic effects, such as amnesia.

Guy H. Montgomery is an expert in the use of hypnosis for the management of symptoms associated with cancer and its treatment. In Chapter 7, he describes a number of strategies for enhancing the common factors that improve response to all psychotherapeutic interventions, including hypnosis treatment. He addresses methods for increasing therapeutic alliance (i.e., being genuine, compassionate, reassuring, and when appropriate, using humor), enhancing perceived control over the experience, negotiating and agreeing on (realistic) treatment goals, maximizing perceived success, encouraging ongoing practice, being empathic, and building positive and realistic outcome expectancies. The approaches he describes are practical and effective.

Consuelo Casula has published extensively on the use of metaphor in psychotherapy. In Chapter 8, she describes how she uses the metaphors patients offer when they describe their presenting problem in the context of therapy. As she states, her chapter "… is *not* on how to create metaphors, but mainly on how to use what the patient brings to the session, while, at the same time, strengthening the therapeutic alliance and entering into greater resonance with the patient's inner world." She notes that clinicians can use metaphors to introduce new ideas and stimulate new ways of thinking about a problem. Indeed, as Erickson says repeatedly, this is the essence of hypnosis: "In hypnosis your task is to guide patients' thinking, to guide the association of ideas along channels that are therapeutic" (p. 127, Erickson, 1983). And again: "… your task is to present ideas to patients in such a fashion that they can respond to them" (p. 20, Erickson, 1985), and "You see, hypnosis doesn't come from mere repetition. It comes from getting your patient to accept an idea and to respond to that idea" (p. 143, Erickson, 1985). Casula elegantly shows how clinicians can use metaphors to do just that.

Shigeru Matsuki is a clinical psychologist with decades of experience in the use of hypnosis to help individuals address a wide variety of psychological and medical problems. In Chapter 9, he describes the principles behind his method for enhancing the patient's responsivity to hypnosis treatment. These principles include: (1) viewing the hypnotic trance as a "space" that lies between the patient and clinician (rather than as something that occurs within the patient); (2) understanding that this space emerges from the interaction between the patient and clinician—both contribute to it; and (3) viewing ideas for suggestions that arise in the clinician as an outcome of this fertile therapeutic space. This space is therefore a powerful tool for helping the patient understand their problem and their resources for managing it. He presents a case, along with portions of a transcript of a treatment session for this case, illustrating how clinicians can apply this approach to improve outcomes.

In Chapter 10, I describe how clinicians can use two foundational psychotherapeutic skills—asking open questions and reflective listening—to identify powerful hypnotic suggestions, which can then be offered both outside of and during more formal hypnosis. The rationale underlying this approach is based on the idea that a patient's automatic cognitive activity can be viewed as "self-suggestions." These influence the subsequent emotional and behavioral responses linked to those self-suggestions. In order to identify the patient's automatic thoughts/self-suggestions that are most useful and could be nurtured, as well as the less-than-useful ones that could benefit from being altered, the clinician needs to listen and observe carefully as the patient discusses his or her presenting problem. Open questions—questions and statements that elicit sentences and paragraphs about a topic—are ideal for this phase. As the clinician hears the self-suggestions that already exist inside the patient, the clinician can test-drive possible hypnotic suggestions and either nurture or change them, as appropriate. This is done by reflecting the ideas expressed by the patient, either as stated or slightly modified to be more helpful. The patient's response to the reflection can then be used to gauge its potential usefulness as a hypnotic suggestion. At the end of the chapter, I provide a transcript of one application of the Hypnotic Reflective Listening approach, as well as a two-year follow-up from the patient.

Enayatollah Shahidi is known internationally for his exceptional teaching in the use of hypnosis for psychotherapy and for leadership in the field. He begins Chapter 11 by noting the common elements that are important to effective psychotherapy across all techniques and approaches, including in the application of clinical hypnosis. He then describes his adaptation of Helen Watkins' Door of Forgiveness technique. In this technique, patients ultimately walk through a door at the end of a corridor as a sign that they have successfully forgiven themselves or someone else who is important in their life. However, before they pass through the door at the end of the hall, they will notice doors on either side of the corridor. They are encouraged to open those doors and to address the issues, events, or memories associated with any lingering feelings that need to be resolved before they are ready to step through the door at the end of the hall. Importantly, this technique can be adapted to help patients address many different issues and treatment goals, by changing it from a Door of Forgiveness to a Door of ... *virtually any goal* (e.g., Health, Comfort, Strength, Confidence). The example transcript he provides includes an induction that illustrates his warm and permissive style. It also demonstrates the language he uses to facilitate the resolution of the issues that are hindering the patient in addressing their treatment goal.

Dorothea Thomaßen is a surgeon who also treats patients presenting with symptoms and conditions influenced by psychological factors. In the 12th and final chapter of this volume, she describes the U-Assessment and Therapeutic Protocol, a specific treatment protocol for helping patients manage symptoms associated with a variety of health and psychological conditions that are interfering with their experience of comfort and well-being. Interestingly, and consistent with the general approach of starting treatment where the patient is now, the clinician first invites the patient to describe his or her experience with a problem in detail. Patients often begin by describing the most intense or bothersome symptoms and move on to less severe symptoms and experiences as they go. For each negative symptom or experience, the clinician then asks the patient to describe its opposite—what the patient would like to experience *instead*. Just going through this process may be enough to activate positive change, by helping patients get in touch with what they wish to experience, and by facilitating their own resources for achieving their well-being goals. In addition the process elicits very specific goals and language which can be incorporated into hypnotic suggestions in subsequent, more formal hypnosis sessions.

The techniques described and modeled by the 11 highly experienced clinicians who have contributed chapters to this volume can be used to address a large number of issues and presenting problems. Moreover, having been vetted and adapted by the authors over many years (often, decades) of clinical experience, the approaches have a great deal of support for their overall efficacy. The reader is encouraged to read about, learn, and practice these techniques, and then to adapt them as needed to make them their own.

References

Erickson, M. H. (1959). Further clinical techniques of hypnosis: Utilization techniques. *American Journal of Clinical Hypnosis, 2,* 3-21.

Erickson, M. H. (1983). In E. L. Rossi, M. O. Ryan, & F. A. Sharp (Eds), *Healing in hypnosis: Volume 1. The seminars, workshops, and lectures of Milton H. Erickson.* New York, NY: Irvington.

Erickson, M. H. (1985). In E. L. Rossi & M. O. Ryan (Eds), *Life reframing in hypnosis: Vol 2. The seminars, workshops, and lectures of Milton H. Erickson.* New York, NY: Irvington.

Erickson, M. H., Rossi, E. L., & Rossi, S. I. (1976). *Hypnotic realities: The induction of clinical hypnosis and forms of indirect suggestion.* New York, NY: Irvington.

Watkins, J. G. (1970). The affect bridge: A hypnoanalytic technique. *International Journal of Clinical and Experimental Hypnosis, 19,* 21-27.

CHAPTER 2

Age Progression as a Therapeutic Modality

Moshe S. Torem

Moshe S. Torem is a psychiatrist certified by the American Board of Psychiatry and Neurology (ABPN). He is a Distinguished Life Fellow of the American Psychiatric Association, Life Fellow of the American Society of Clinical Hypnosis, and Life Fellow of the Society for Clinical and Experimental Hypnosis. Dr. Torem served as president of the International Society for the Study of Trauma and Dissociation (ISSTD) and the American Society of Clinical Hypnosis (ASCH). Currently, Dr. Torem serves as professor of psychiatry at Northeast Ohio Medical University. In addition, Dr. Torem has published numerous articles and book chapters in the fields of psychiatry, hypnosis, integrative mind-body medicine, and health. He has provided lectures and workshops to professionals in the USA and throughout the world. Dr. Torem has also been in clinical practice providing guidance and treatment for people seeking assistance for a variety of conditions such as: anxiety, depression, eating disorders, insomnia, habit disorders, smoking control, weight control, autoimmune disorders, and preparation for medical procedures and surgery. Moreover, Dr. Torem has also provided successful guidance and help using this age progression modality to students and workers in passing examinations and preparing for important interviews. Dr. Torem is known for his practical approaches utilizing age-progression procedures with and without formal hypnosis as an important and unique contribution to the field of hypnosis and therapeutic imagery.

*   *   *

*Man has his future within him, dynamically
active in this present moment*

—Abraham Maslow (1968)

About 30 years ago, I first described an age-progression procedure I called, "Back from the Future" (Torem, 1989, 1990, 1992a). This therapeutic technique is based on the utilization of age-progression interventions enhanced by hypnosis. The foundation of this procedure is based on the notion that is eloquently expressed by Paul Watzlawick who stated that, "...the future (not the past) determines the present; the prophecy of the event leads to the event of the prophecy" (Watzlawick, 1993, p. 13).

Using the Back from the Future intervention requires an understanding of and familiarity with the patient's personal history, current condition, and life circumstances. A discussion is held with the patient about a desired future event representing a better, healthier, desired, or at least acceptable setting in his/her life. The therapist co-creates and specifies with the patient such a desired best possible outcome event/situation, acting as a coach who provides the boundaries of the future-focused experience and assists in finding an appropriate balance between desired possibility and realistic plausibility.

Once the outcome is identified, the patient is guided into a state of hypnotic trance, and an age progression is hypnotically facilitated by "mental time-travel" into a specific place and time in the future. This future reality is hypnotically enhanced by suggestions focused on experiencing the future with all five senses (visual, auditory, tactile, olfactory, and gustatory). In addition, the experiences are enhanced by ego-strengthening suggestions as described by Frederick and McNeal (1999), Hartland (1965, 1971), and Torem (1990).

In the Back from the Future procedure, the focus is on suggestions for positive thinking and pleasant feelings of joy and satisfaction in reaching a solution to a specific problem, attaining comfort and relief from severe pain or other painful symptoms, or experiencing a specific desirable future event such as: celebrating a graduation, starting a new job, completing an important project, celebrating the birth of a child or grandchild, celebrating a relationship anniversary, moving into a new house, or celebrating one's retirement, etc. This focus is accompanied by suggestions for a sense of health, strength, accomplishment and resilience and a sense of inner resourcefulness and creativity in coping with life's stresses. The patient is then instructed to store these experiences, sensations, positive feelings, images, and sense of accomplishment and to internalize and encode these consciously and subconsciously. Then, the patient is hypnotically guided back from the future into the present at the here and now. Patients are told that these positive images, sensations, feelings, and experiences are special gifts that they bring back with them on their mental time-trip from the future into the present and that these gifts will guide them on conscious and subconscious levels on their journey of healing and recovery.

When the patient is no longer in the formal hypnotic state, a brief discussion is conducted about the patient's experience.

At this point, I actively listen to the patient's report. This is followed by a homework assignment in which the patient is asked to write about the experience and to describe what it was like to take such a voyage into the future and experience a solution to the problem. This writing assignment can alternatively be requested while the patient is in a state of hypnotic trance as a gentle suggestion.

The patient is asked to bring the written assignment to the next session and to read it to me. It is not uncommon that the initial verbal narrative about the future-focused experience includes verbs that are grammatically past tense. For example, a patient verbally describing the experience of a future event, when her (currently) ten-year-old son is participating in the ceremony of graduating from high school at the age of 18, may say, "I saw my son all dressed up in cap and gown as he was walking to receive his high school diploma. I felt so proud when they called his name; later he gave me a hug and a kiss and I could smell the scent of his after-shave lotion."

In my clinical experience, individuals who spontaneously engage in describing their Back from the Future experience using past tense verbs usually have better outcomes with this type of future-focused intervention. The symptoms of futurelessness, helplessness, and hopelessness are significantly reduced and are replaced by a sense of new hope, inner strength, resourcefulness, self-mastery, and belief in one's recovery.

In the book *Inner Strengths,* co-authored by Frederick and McNeal (1999), the authors provide a descriptive commentary on the Back from the Future procedure stating:

> Torem's technique is extremely powerful for many reasons. One is that a view of the future that is enhanced with sensory components of sight,

hearing, touch, and so on may become a true vivification. That is that the patient may actually relive the experience in quite a vivid way. This aspect of the experience is projective/evocative in that it ignites combinations of inner resources that manifest themselves in the experience. In addition to this, potent direct suggestion is added at a time when the patient is highly 'programmable' because of her deep involvement in a hypnotic experience. The additional direct suggestion that she is bringing back a manifold of gifts with her into the present that can work at deep levels of mind brings resources from the future into the present. The patient's participation in discussion, self-hypnosis, and writing and reading about the experience reinforce it further. (pp. 112-113)

Since 1990, I have reported on the use of this Back from the Future procedure in the treatment of depression (Torem, 2006, 2017b), the treatment of eating disorders (Torem, 1991a, 2001, 2017c), the control of self-inflicted violence (Torem, 1995, 1997), for enhancing ego-strengthening (Torem, 1990), for enhancing desired best outcome with therapeutic imagery (Torem, 1992c), for enhancing internal integration of compartmentalized and separated ego states (Torem & Gainer, 1995), for the treatment of hyperemesis gravidarum (Torem, 1991b, 1994), for preparing students and others for a written examination or job interview (Torem, 2005), for the treatment of autoimmune disorders (Torem, 2007, 2017a), for pediatric functional disorders (Torem, 2014), and for a variety of interventions in the arena of integrative health (Torem, 2017d).

Moreover, the successful utilization of the Back from the Future procedure has also been also reported by Stanton (1994), in his application of sports imagery with hypnosis. Jensen (2011, 2017) reported on the value of using age progression in the treatment of patients with chronic pain. More recently, Bonshtein and Torem (2017), reported on the use of a modified version of the Back from the Future procedure as a "forward affect bridge" in the practice of psychotherapy.

Transcript

The following transcript is a representative version of the Back from the Future technique as it was applied in the case of an individual who consciously and subconsciously believed that he would die at the age his father was when his father passed away. This fear is not uncommon and deals with basic issues of identity such as: Who am I? Is my fate set genetically? Am I a replica of my father/mother? Who shall I become? The age-progression procedure and strategy is an excellent intervention that allows patients to internalize a desirable experienced future. This experience acts as a subconscious hook that is experienced in a trance logic process as a future that already happened.

Clinician: Go ahead and put yourself in a comfortable position as you are sitting in this chair with your hands on your lap. You may hold your hands with your palms upward, or down touching your lap; you may choose whatever makes you more comfortable... you may even change this position in a few minutes if you wish to do so.

[Giving the patient a choice of how to position his or her body is a good example of a participatory approach to the process of

entering a different state of mind. It also results in better
cooperation.]

As we discussed earlier, you informed me that your father
passed away from a heart condition at the age of 45. As you
are now getting close to this age you have begun wondering
if you too would develop a heart condition, just like your
father did.

However, as we discussed earlier, even though you loved
your father, you have begun to recognize the fact that you
are not a replica of your father; you are different and
separate from your father, and you in fact may very well live
a full and meaningful long life. You have begun to realize
that you may love your father without becoming your
father.

> *[This suggestion sets the foundation for a disidentification*
> *from the father without also needing to stop loving the father.*
> *This concept will make it easier for this individual to accept*
> *and experience something new and different in the*
> *future—something his father never lived to experience.]*

In this context we discussed a special event in the future; a
party celebrating your 80th birthday. So, go ahead and take
a deep breath... and as you slowly exhale... let your eyelids
close. As you keep breathing in... and out... at your own
pace. ... Each time you exhale you let all the stress and
tension leave your body, and as you inhale you bring in
calmness and tranquility... to replace the stress and tension
that have left.

> *[I say the words in... and out... matched with the patient's*
> *rhythm of breathing. The word in... is matched with inhaling*
> *the breath and the word out... is matched with the act of*
> *exhaling. This is a good example of "pacing," which sets the*

foundation for leading. It provides suggestions for letting go of stress and tension coupled with the act of exhaling and provides suggestions for internalizing calmness and tranquility coupled with the act of inhaling.]

As you continue to breathe comfortably at your own pace, notice how this state of tranquility is slowly spreading from your head down to your toes, top to bottom, inside out and outside in. You may now open a new channel of concentration, whereby you experience yourself at a special event. It is the celebration of your 80th birthday. This event takes place at an ocean beach resort of your choice.

[The exact place, age, and specific event were chosen by the patient in the detailed discussion we had before the formal hypnotic session began. It is very important to note that it is the clinician's responsibility to actively participate in these choices, guiding the patient to select realistically plausible events and to avoid events that have no chance of being realized.]

Your wife and the rest of your family are with you; as are your children, grandchildren, cousins, and some special close friends. Notice the decorations in the well-lit, large room... the beautiful fresh flowers, in their special vases. As the guests arrive and come to greet you, look at their glowing faces... their loving eyes. ... As the hugs take place, notice the touch of their lips on your cheek... the scent of their perfume... the texture of their skin... and their clothes. Your wife is standing by your side, at times holding your hand, at times touching your face and looking at you with her loving eyes. Listen to the nice words people say to you, appreciating the invitation to participate in celebrating your 80th birthday.

[The suggestions given here are experienced by the patient with the visual sense (seeing), the auditory sense (hearing), the tactile sense (touching and being touched), the olfactory sense (smelling the scent of flowers, perfume, or food), and the gustatory sense (experiencing the taste of food or drinks). At this point, I may ask the patient to describe in their own words what he/she sees, hears, smells, etc. This method reinforces the experience and acts as verification for me that we are on the right track and are ready to focus on the additional suggestions.]

Now, the time has come to sit at the table for the special birthday meal. All the participants raise their glasses with a special blessing to you on this birthday. You can experience the unique aroma of your favorite wine as it touches your taste buds on your palate. Experience the taste of the freshly baked rolls, just the way you like them. Enjoy the taste of the food. And as you chew and swallow this delicious food, you also internalize the feelings of joy, pleasure, and love you feel towards your friends and the love that is coming from them to you.

[Choosing to focus on experiencing a meal and the act of eating, chewing, and swallowing is very important; this serves as a metaphor for the process of internalization of the whole experience, including thoughts, feelings, and behavior.]

Before the dessert is served, members of your family and friends step up to the podium to talk about you and their appreciation of you and the unique relationship they have with you. Listen to the wonderful words from your wife, children, and grandchildren.

[Here the focus is on the auditory sense; the act of hearing and listening.]

Now, the time has come for your special words of appreciation. Notice how fluent your speech is; your words are laced with humor and a smile. ... Notice how good you feel about yourself and the whole event. ... Dessert is served, fresh fruit, delicious cake, and warm drinks of tea or coffee.

[Again, seizing the opportunity of internalizing the experience coupled with the act of chewing and swallowing (incorporation).]

Now, take the time to internalize this whole experience... to encode it in your mind consciously and subconsciously and let it be available to you any time you need this experience, as a reminder of how much promise and joy are waiting for you in the future. As you are getting ready to return to the present day, place, and time, bring back with you these wonderful experiences as special gifts from the future.

[Hence the name of this special age-progression procedure; Back from the Future.]

Let these experiences guide you every day, every hour of the day... infusing you with hope, joy, and general optimism about your life. Now, when you are ready... go ahead and take a deep breath. And as you exhale, experience yourself coming back from the future to the present day and time. As you refocus your thoughts, your eyelids open, your vision comes back into focus, you are becoming alert, awake, and fully oriented to the place, where we are now, the day of... *[here I mention the day of the week, the date, the month, and the year]*. Look at me; can you clearly see my face? What is my name? What is today's date? How are you feeling? Now that

you are fully reoriented, please remember to bring with you to your next session a written essay describing your whole experience and how it has affected you.

[These are suggestions for dehypnotizing and refocusing the patient to the here and now. A discussion follows asking the patient to describe the experience, and also engaging in a discussion about the present reality and verifying the patient's orientation and plans for the rest of the day. A follow-up appointment is scheduled. In the follow-up session the patient is asked to read the essay. Frequently, patients use the past tense when describing their experience. This typically implies that the experience was internalized.]

Conclusion

This chapter reviews the benefits of using an age progression, future-focused procedure called Back from the Future. This procedure may be utilized for a variety of conditions and situations. For example, in preparing patients for elective surgery. The potential benefits of this procedure far outweigh any potential draw-backs, such as the time it takes to work with patients on a one to one level in utilizing this procedure. I believe that hypnotically enhanced future-focused imagery should be used more often in preparing patients for elective surgery.

The essential elements involve experiencing (in all five senses) a desired plausible future. This experience has an empowering ripple effect (Spiegel & Linn, 1969) on self-perceptions and activities of day-to-day living. Expectancy (Kirsch, 1999, 2001) is also an important element in realizing a desirable experienced future. The mechanism of self-fulfilling prophecies (Watzlawick, 1984) may well be another factor involved in the realizing effect of the Back from the Future age-progression procedure.

The specific transcript (used as an example) in this chapter is designed to illustrate the principles of internalizing a desired positive future: the experiences are internalized and encoded mentally and physically with suggestions to this effect. Individuals who spontaneously use the past tense in describing their experiences are those who have successfully internalized their desired future.

References

Bonshtein, U., & Torem, M. (2017). Forward Affect Bridge. *International Journal of Clinical and Experimental Hypnosis, 65,* 43-51.

Frederick, C., & McNeal, S. (1999). *Inner strengths.* Mahwah, NJ: Lawrence Erlbaum Associates.

Hartland, J. (1965). The value of ego-strengthening procedures prior to direct symptom removal under hypnosis. *American Journal of Clinical Hypnosis, 8,* 89-93.

Hartland, J. (1971). Further observation of the use of ego-strengthening techniques. *American Journal of Clinical Hypnosis, 14,* 1-8.

Jensen, M. P. (2011). *Hypnosis for chronic pain management: Therapist guide.* Oxford, UK: Oxford University Press.

Jensen, M. P. (2017). Pain management, chronic pain. In G. R. Elkins (Ed.), *Handbook of medical and psychological hypnosis: Foundations, applications, and professional issues* (pp. 341-360). New York, NY: Springer.

Kirsch, I. (1999). *How expectancies shape experience.* Washington, DC: American Psychological Association.

Kirsch, I. (2001). The Response Set Theory of Hypnosis: Expectancy and physiology. *American Journal of Clinical Hypnosis, 44,* 69-73.

Maslow, A. H. (1968). *Toward a psychology of being*. New York, NY: D. van Nostrand.

Spiegel, H., & Linn, L. (1969). The "ripple effect" following adjunct hypnosis in analytic psychotherapy. *American Journal of Psychiatry, 126*, 53-58.

Stanton, H. E. (1994). Sports imagery and hypnosis: A potent mix. *Australian Journal of Clinical & Experimental Hypnosis, 22*, 119-124.

Torem, M. S. (1989). Recognition and management of dissociative regressions. *Hypnos, 16*, 197-213.

Torem, M. S. (1990). Ego strengthening. In D. C. Hammond (Ed.), *Handbook of hypnotic suggestions and metaphors* (pp. 110-112). New York: WW Norton.

Torem, M. S. (1991a). Eating Disorders. In W. C. Wester & D. J. O'Grady (Eds.), *Clinical hypnosis with children* (pp. 230-255). New York: Brunner/Mazel.

Torem, M. S. (1991b, March). *Hypnotherapeutic techniques in the treatment of hyperemesis gravidarum*. Paper presented at the American Society of Clinical Hypnosis Annual meeting, St. Louis, MO.

Torem, M. S. (1992a). "Back from the future": A powerful age progression technique. *American Journal of Clinical Hypnosis, 35*, 81-88.

Torem, M. S. (1992b). Therapeutic imagery enhanced by hypnosis. *Psychiatric Medicine, 10*, 1-12.

Torem, M. S. (1994). Hypnotherapeutic techniques in the treatment of hyperemesis gravidarum. *American Journal of Clinical Hypnosis, 37*, 1-11.

Torem, M. S. (1995). A practical approach in the treatment of self-inflicted violence. *Journal of Holistic Nursing, 13*, 37-53.

Torem, M. S., & Gainer, M. J. (1995). The center-core: Imagery for experiencing the unifying self. *Hypnos, 22*, 125-131.

Torem, M. S. (1997). Diagnostic and therapeutic use of "inner advisor" imagery. *Hypnos, 24,* 107-109.

Torem, M. S. (2001). Eating disorders: Anorexia and bulimia. In G. D. Burrows, R. O. Stanley, & P. B. Bloom (Eds.), *International handbook of clinical hypnosis* (pp. 205-219). New York, NY: John Wiley & Sons.

Torem, M. S. (2005, October). *Future Focused Hypnotherapy.* Paper presented at the Annual Scientific Meeting of the Society for Clinical and Experimental Hypnosis, Charleston, SC.

Torem, M. S. (2006). Treating depression: A remedy from the future. In M. Yapko (Ed.), *Hypnosis and treating depression: Applications in clinical practice* (pp. 97-119). New York, NY: Routledge.

Torem, M. S. (2007). Mind-body hypnotic imagery in the treatment of auto-immune disorders. *American Journal of Clinical Hypnosis, 50,* 157-170.

Torem, M. S. (2014). Guided imagery for functional disorders. In R. Anbar (Ed.), *Functional symptoms in pediatric disease: A clinical guide* (pp. 319-33). New York, NY: Springer.

Torem, M. S. (2017a). Autoimmune disorders. In G. R. Elkins (Ed.), *Handbook of medical and psychological hypnosis* (pp. 169-177). New York, NY: Springer.

Torem, M. S. (2017b). Depression. In G. R. Elkins (Ed.), *Handbook of medical and psychological hypnosis* (pp. 505-521). New York, NY: Springer.

Torem, M. S. (2017c). Eating disorders. In G. R. Elkins (Ed.), *Handbook of medical and psychological hypnosis* (pp. 523-534). New York, NY: Springer.

Torem, M. S. (2017d). Future-focused therapeutic strategies for integrative health. *International Journal of Clinical and Experimental Hypnosis, 65,* 353-378.

Watzlawick, P. (1984). Self-fulfilling prophecies. In P. Watzlawick (Ed.), *The invented reality* (pp. 95-116). New York, NY: WW Norton.

Watzlawick, P. (1993), If you desire to see learn how to act. In G. Nardone & P. Watzlawick (Eds.), *The art of change* (pp. 1-13). San Francisco, CA: Jossey-Bass.

For Further Reading ...

Benson, H. (1996). *Timeless healing: The power and biology of belief.* New York, NY: Scribner.

De Shazer, S. (1985). *Keys to solution in brief therapy.* New York, NY: WW Norton.

Elkins, G. R. (Ed.). (2017). *Handbook of medical and psychological hypnosis: Foundations, applications, and professional issues.* New York, NY: Springer.

Erickson, M. (1954). Pseudo-orientation in time as a hypnotherapeutic procedure. *International Journal of Clinical and Experimental Hypnosis, 2,* 161-283.

Frankl, V. E. (1956). From psychotherapy to logotherapy. *Pastoral Psychology, 7,* 56-60.

Frankl, V. E. (1959). *Man's search for meaning.* New York, NY: Simon and Schuster.

Frederick, C., & Phillips, M. (1992). The use of age progression as interventions with acute psychosomatic conditions. *American Journal of Clinical Hypnosis, 35,* 89-98.

Hammond, D.C. (1990). Age-progression. In D.C. Hammond (Ed.), *Handbook of hypnotic suggestions and metaphors* (pp. 515-516). New York, NY: WW Norton.

Havens, R. A. (1985). *The wisdom of Milton H. Erickson.* New York, NY: Irvington Publishers.

Havens, R. A. (1986). Posthypnotic predetermination of therapeutic progress. *American Journal of Clinical Hypnosis, 28,* 258-262.

Jussim, L. (1986). Self-fulfilling prophecies: A theoretical and integrative review. *Psychological Review, 93,* 429-445.

Kekecs, Z., & Varga, K. (2013). Positive suggestion techniques in somatic medicine: A review of the empirical studies. *Interventional Medicine and Applied Science, 5,* 101-111.

Kessler, R. S., & Miller, S. D. (1995). The use of a future time frame in psychotherapy with and without hypnosis. *American Journal of Clinical Hypnosis, 38,* 39-46.

Kirsch, I. (1999). *How expectancies shape experience.* Washington, DC: American Psychological Association.

Lazarus, A. (1984). *In the mind's eye: The power of imagery for personal enrichment.* New York, NY: Guilford Press.

Lombardo, T. (2007). The evolution and psychology of future consciousness. *Journal of Future Studies 12,* 1-24.

Melges, F. T. (1972). Future oriented psychotherapy. *American Journal of Psychotherapy, 26,* 22-33.

Melges, F. T. (1982). *Time and the inner future.* New York, NY: John Wiley.

Napier, N. J. (1990). *Recreating yourself: Help for adult children of dysfunctional families.* New York, NY: WW Norton.

O'Hanlon, W. H., & Weiner-Davis, M. (1989). *In search of solutions.* New York, NY: WW Norton.

Patterson, D. R. (2010). *Clinical hypnosis for pain control.* New York, NY: American Psychological Association.

Phillips, M. & Frederick, C. (1992). The use of hypnotic age progressions as prognostic, ego-strengthening, and integrating techniques. *American Journal of Clinical Hypnosis, 35,* 99-108.

Sools, A. & Mooren, J. H. (2012). Towards narrative futuring in psychology: Becoming resilient by imaging the future. *Graduate Journal of Social Science, 9,* 203-226.

Spiegel, H. & Spiegel, D. (1978). *Trance and treatment: Clinical use of hypnosis.* New York, NY: Basic Books.

Thomson, L., (2017). Pre-Surgery. In Gary R. Elkins (Ed.), *Handbook of medical and psychological hypnosis; Foundations, applications, and professional issues* (pp. 379-385). New York, NY: Springer.

Torem, M. S. (1992). Hypnosis: Lingering myths and established facts. *Psychiatric Medicine, 10,* 1-11.

Torem, M. S. (1996). Diagnostic and therapeutic use of 'inner advisor' imagery. *The Milton H. Erickson Foundation Newsletter, 16,* 3.

Torem, M. S. (2010). The central role of suggestion in all clinical encounters including psychoanalysis. *Neuropsychoanalysis, 12,* 43-46.

Varga, K. (2013). Suggestive techniques connected to medical interventions. *Interventional Medicine and Applied Science, 5,* 95-100.

Watzlawick, P. (1993). *The language of change: Elements of therapeutic communication.* New York, NY: WW Norton.

Watzlawick, P., Bavelas, J. B., Jackson, D. D., & O'Hanlon, B. (2011a). *Pragmatics of human communication: A study of interactional patterns, pathologies and paradoxes.* New York, NY: WW Norton.

Watzlawick, P., Weakland, J. H., & Fisch, R. (2011b). *Change: Principles of problem formation and problem resolution.* New York, NY: WW Norton.

Yapko, M.D. (1986). Depression: Diagnostic frameworks and therapeutic strategies. In M.D. Yapko (Ed.), *Hypnotic and strategic interventions: Principles & practice.* (pp. 241-242). New York, NY: Brunner/Mazel.

Yapko, M. (1997). *Breaking the patterns of depression.* New York, NY: Random House/Doubleday.

Yapko, M. (2002). The power of vision as an antidepressant: Rethinking the focus of therapy. In J. Zeig (Ed.), *Brief therapy: Lasting impressions* (pp. 63–78). Phoenix, AZ: Milton H. Erickson Foundation Press.

Yapko, M. (2006). *Hypnosis and treating depression: Application in clinical practice.* New York, NY: Routledge.

Yapko, M. (2010a). Hypnosis in the treatment of depression: An overdue approach for encouraging skillful mood management. *International Journal of Clinical and Experimental Hypnosis, 58,* 137–146.

Yapko, M. (2010b). Hypnotically catalyzing experiential learning across treatments for depression: Actions can speak louder than moods. *International Journal of Clinical and Experimental Hypnosis, 58,* 186–201

Zilbergeld, B. & Lazarus, A.A. (1987). *Mind power: Getting what you want through mental training.* Boston, MA: Little, Brown & Co.

CHAPTER 3

A Practical Approach to
Age Regression Therapy

Michael Schekter

Michael Schekter is an independent medical doctor and specialist in clinical psychiatry and psychotherapy in Lausanne, Switzerland. Interested in promoting hypnosis, he teaches and supervises health professionals nationally and internationally, and also facilitates workshops at national and international congresses. He is a committee member of the Swiss Medical Society for Hypnosis, is on the Board of Directors of the European Society of Hypnosis, and is a long-standing member of the International Society of Hypnosis. He is especially interested in techniques that contribute to lasting, positive, psychological, and physical changes acquired during age regression therapy and Four Squares Therapy, which is a modified version of an eye movement desensitization and reprocessing protocol for use by hypnotherapists.

*   *   *

I am delighted to be contributing a chapter to this volume. When I was invited to participate, it made me think of my beginning years in hypnosis, when a small group of courageous and dedicated American health professionals—experts in hypnotherapy—crossed the ocean to share their know-how with us in Switzerland and in other European countries. My encounter with Deborah Ross and her model of age regression therapy, in particular, led me to open a door in psychotherapy, which I have never closed.

The age regression technique has inspired many therapists, such as Pierre Janet in the 19th century in France. In the 20th century, Milton Erickson and his followers continued to develop these approaches. Today, many hypnotherapists use this technique throughout the world.

I use this technique regularly in my private practice and teach it to therapists in workshops. This approach leads to major psychological and psychosomatic changes. During therapy, the therapist uses his or her medical and psychological knowledge, helps create a therapeutic alliance, and proposes and applies trance techniques with the patient's acceptance and active participation. The patient discovers how to exploit his or her inherent intuitive capacities and to acquire new ways to act and to be. The explicit common goal is to liberate the patient from blocked, frozen, or negative repetitive responses and disturbing symptoms and to replace these with more resourceful, adaptive responses. The original version of the technique has been repeatedly modified. Therapeutic experiences with patients and other encounters with hypnotherapists continue to contribute to this evolution.

After birth, the individual—with his or her unique genetic makeup—interacts in a complex manner with family members, peers, and the environment within a defined society. In spite of the therapist's benevolent and nonjudgmental relationship and professional skills for gathering information, the therapist understands that it is practically impossible to know all of the situations in the patient's life that led to trauma and at what moment the most impactful traumas occurred. During the age regression approach, the patient and the therapist are witnesses to the patient's important subjective negative experiences, with their associated painful emotions and disturbing body feelings; all of which are linked to today's psychological and psychosomatic symptoms. As the therapist-patient team explores these negative past experiences, they can create new, positive ones, which then become today's resources (with their favorable thoughts, emotions and body feelings).

When I propose age regression therapy to patients, I start by presenting an understandable model that explains the creation of their presenting symptoms. I say something like:

Therapist: We might say that when confronted with a strong emotional experience, our natural defense system automatically reacts and binds the disturbing negative energy. This permits us to continue to function in everyday life and to remain active. However, sometimes the emotional experiences are so strong or overwhelming that the automatic binding system can only be partially successful. Certain psychological conditions and symptoms are the end result of these partially successful solutions. We codify some of them as traumatic stress syndrome, phobias, obsessive-compulsive disorders, conversions, somatoform pain conditions, and psychosomatic illnesses. Unfortunately, one's life can be limited by these symptoms, and they can interfere with the ability to adapt to life's constant changes.

I ask the patient if he or she would like to try a method which could help the intuitive unconscious find a better solution to dealing with the trauma. Then the old ways could be replaced by new ways. I remind the patient that he or she is more experienced now than "back then," when it all started. If the patient expresses interest, I propose the age regression method to promote this change.

Before sharing the protocol, I would like to describe certain basic conditions necessary for its successful use. As in all consultations, the patient comes with immediate difficulties and symptoms. A case history is taken based on the therapist's therapeutic approach. The patient's difficulties as well as his or her resources should be noted. The dates of appearance of the presenting symptoms help the patient realize that he or she has not always had the presenting symptoms and underlines the theoretical model that emotional situations which become overwhelming can lead to the appearance of symptoms at a certain moment. This evaluation and discussion also permits the establishment of the therapeutic alliance.

Clinical hypnosis is goal oriented. What does the patient need and want to change? Can age regression therapy help to address these needs and facilitate the desired changes? There are two major goals in this approach:

1. By using a *positive* age regression protocol, patients can identify and reinforce a specific resource within themselves, such as strength, a sense of confidence, or an ability to experience calm. Patients accomplish this by regressing to a younger age when they had a bit of the desired quality. At that age, the younger, regressed self re-lives this experience along with its thoughts, bodily sensations, and emotions. The younger self can then bring this resource back to the present-day self and integrate it. This resource is then available to the patient when needed, to deal with everyday challenges; for example, to have the confidence to pass an exam. A variation of this technique can be applied to pathological mourning. The patient regresses to a younger self in order to live a positive past experience

with the beloved deceased person. The regressed younger self and the deceased share this past positive moment; for example, by expressing their thoughts and feelings or their mutual caring and love. These positive thoughts, with their attached body sensations and emotions, are brought back to the current self and integrated within the patient today. This experience fills the empty space created by the "apparently" lost relationship and can become a constant reminder of the love and care linked to the deceased person.

2. In *negative* age regression, the patient deals with past traumatic experiences that are linked to the origins of his or her presenting symptoms. This protocol offers a secure way for the patient to access the past and to help the younger self confront the ongoing, unsuccessfully resolved traumatic situation. The patient encourages the younger self to create a new and successful scenario. When the younger self returns to the present and integrates the insights and the experience of successful coping, the symptoms usually improve or even disappear. Brain plasticity allows the new, successful scenario to replace the old.

In the following pages, I illustrate the use of age regression by presenting the transcript of a session using the negative age regression protocol. Although the steps described might appear complicated on first reading, the actual use of the protocol during therapy is quite easy to apply after some training and guidance.

When teaching this approach, I distribute a written protocol. I ask the learning therapists to follow the protocol until they have assimilated the different steps. This permits them to help their patient experience important personal changes while limiting the potential for missteps. As therapists gain more experience with the protocol, they will adapt it to fit their personal therapeutic approach and personality.

The Negative Age Regression Protocol:
Step-by-Step

1. Target: Identify the target situation and evaluate the patient's subjective level (or "unit") of disturbance (SUD).

2. Safe place: The patient goes to and experiences his or her "safe place" (previously established).

3. Age regression: The patient regresses in age to the *oldest* (ideally, "first") linked past experience by using a modified affect bridge (originally described by Watkins, 1971), represented by the body feelings and emotions previously determined in the target. This voyage follows the path of the patient's associated memories.

4. Observation: The patient observes the ongoing past experience of his or her younger self and describes it to the therapist.

5. Re-parenting: Usually, the patient provides a persistent, loving, caring, and unconditional parental relationship to the younger self, even if only separated by a small age difference. However, sometimes the younger self is more able than the actual patient and does not need or accept the patient's reassurance. As a matter of fact, the younger self might even bring reassurance and security to the current-self patient.

6. Evocation and creating the new resource: The patient asks the younger self to explain in his or her own words what is happening at that moment in that place. Then, the younger self is asked to find a better solution to the problem and experience it.

7. Bringing back the resource: The younger self is asked to grow up to the patient's size and age today, bringing back with him the new way, with its positive thoughts, and body and emotional sensations. While voyaging back, the patient is asked to pass through all the important moments in his or her life and to "let change that which changes" during this trip.

8. Integration: Having accomplished this growth, the younger self is invited to integrate his or herself into the patient.

9. Post-hypnotic suggestion: The post-hypnotic suggestion that "positive changes will continue without any other effort or action... in the seconds, in the hours, and days to come" is offered.

10. Return to the safe place: Then the patient is asked to go again to his or her safe place.

11. Return to the therapist's office: The patient is then invited to return to the therapist's office, and a discussion follows with the patient about the experience.

12. Debriefing: The next session is scheduled. During that visit, the therapist invites the patient to reflect on the changes in the patient's life that he or she has noticed since the last session.

Case Study: Belinda

Belinda (the patient's name is changed here to maintain confidentiality) is the elder of two children. She describes her mother as "egocentric" and "nasty." The patient's mother worked with the patient's father in a small, family-owned hotel and pub. Belinda married early. When she was 19 she had an automobile accident. Her husband (at the time) was driving and hit a bus. Belinda, as a passenger, went headfirst through the car windshield. Although shocked by the accident, and despite some physical wounds (especially cuts on her face), she was able to recover.

Following her divorce, she led a successful professional life as a full-time accountant. She remarried and had one daughter with her second husband. She came to see me after being involved in two car accidents separated by only three months. She had been the driver in both of these accidents. In both accidents, her car was hit from behind and totaled.

Following the second accident, she began to have severe post-traumatic stress disorder (PTSD) symptoms, including intense fear, flash-backs, nightmares, intense anxiety when exposed to perception cues such as hearing police sirens, feeling cold air, and suddenly feeling someone behind her— provoking a startle reaction. She developed avoidance strategies which limited her ability to adapt to everyday life. The symptoms were severe enough that she became unable to work, go out of her home onto a busy street, or drive.

Initially, I treated her with hypnosis using a variety of techniques including positive and negative age regression therapy and psychotherapy; however, recovery was slow. It became even slower after the insurance company that was providing workers' compensation made it clear they were not satisfied with her rate of recovery and asked for an outside expert evaluation.

That expert concluded that the patient did not have significant symptoms, which further traumatized the patient. She did not feel that she was able to make herself heard. In spite of this, she continued to be motivated by a strong desire to heal and improve her quality of life. She continued in her therapy and returned to part-time work as well as to driving her car again.

Several years later, *another* accident occurred, and in the same manner as the last two, with the patient's car being totaled. At that point, I proposed, and the patient agreed to, the four squares technique, which is a modified eye movement desensitization and reprocessing protocol (Oswald & Schekter, 2012). After only three sessions, her symptoms resolved.

Nevertheless, four years later she returned to see me. At that time, she reported a return of her driving phobia, similar to that which she had developed after her car accidents years earlier. She explained that her beloved brother had died two months prior to our new meeting. She clearly expressed anger towards her mother, who had taken the inheritance money left to Belinda by her brother. During our discussion Belinda stated that she had been involved in another car accident two years prior to this recent office visit, but this did not result in major symptoms. She said that her actual symptoms had started about two months before the visit to my office. This onset seemed to coincide with her brother's death and her mother's selfish action. We decided to use the negative age regression protocol.

Step 1: Target

Determine the difficult situation to be treated and transform it into a target.

Therapist: So, can you tell me what is the most difficult for you? What is happening?

Patient: When I start driving; like today, before coming to see you, I start to feel bad. When I drive I am always surprised that I get *there [the destination]*; that no one has crashed into me or that I've not seen or been in an accident.

Therapist: What about working on the moment that you just talked about, when you're going to get into your car to come to my office?

Patient: That'd be okay. *[The patient closes her eyes.]*

Therapist: Can you just imagine, this moment now—maybe you can see it, maybe you can feel it, maybe you can hear what is happening—just signal when you are there. ... Good. Now, just tell me what you're feeling in your body sitting *here in my office.*

Patient: I'm feeling nervous, my mouth has gone dry. I'm feeling tension in my chest. My heart is beating faster. There is tension in my hands, as though I'm clinging on to something. My legs feel a bit weak.

Therapist: What emotions are you feeling at this point, *here in my office?*

Patient: I'm apprehensive and worried about the traffic and feeling as if someone will crash into me.

Therapist: As if you were in danger?

Patient: Yes.

Therapist: When you're imagining this, here in my office, at this moment, how much is this disturbing you? The scale is between 0 (it doesn't disturb me at all) up to 10 (the most disturbance that I could experience in my life).

Patient: Eight [*Subjective Units of Disturbance-SUD.*]

Therapist: That's a lot. Now, you can erase it all, as on a blackboard in school. Take a deep breath, open your eyes, and come back here.

> [*It is essential to cut off from this momentary confrontation with the traumatic experience by returning to today's safety and reality in the therapist's office.*]

Would you be willing to do something about it now?

Patient: Yes. I forgot to say that I had another accident again two years ago. Also, when my husband drives, it's difficult for me, because we often have a lot of near misses…

Therapist: When did all this start to bother you again?

Patient: About two months ago. I became sensitive to the sounds of police cars and the whoosh sound of the traffic on the motorway. It's taken away my liberty and independence.

> [*The setting up of the target is fundamental and usually takes one session. When I ask the patient to imagine the difficult situation, I create a light, conversational trance state. I ask her to evaluate her bodily feelings and emotions, here and now, in the armchair, in my office. This state represents the residual effect of the trauma, still present today. It is understood that the unconscious mind and the automatic defense system have already dealt with the traumatic moment, although only partially. The feelings and*

emotions are usually less intense now than they were at their origin. Many patients are not able to access their underlying traumatic state. Over time, many have put on a mask of improved health. They may not even realize the ongoing intensity of these feelings beneath the surface. When they establish the target, they realize that they need treatment. (Be sure to finish with the safe place before they go home.)]

Step 2: Safe place

[The patient's safe place should have already been established. If not, the therapist should take the time to do so at this step.]

Therapist: Do you remember your safe place? Well, you can just go there for a moment to let yourself relax the way you already know how to—and maybe you can just let go of those tensions that you don't need any more by breathing them out; and in that created space breathe in fresh air full of energy... which can circulate wherever you need it... allowing you to go more easily to your very special place of comfort, relaxation, good feelings, well protected, and secure... when you get there just let me know... by allowing the head to nod, or allowing a finger to lift—any finger of any hand—or by letting the voice say so out-loud.

Patient: Okay.

Therapist: So now just give yourself a moment, maybe two minutes of clock time in your special place. Now, when you're ready to go a bit further just let me know.

Patient: *[Patient takes about two minutes, and says,]* **Okay.**

[The ability to use the safe place technique to stabilize is a pre-requisite. I start from the safe place and finish at the safe place. This diminishes the risk of re-traumatization, which

might lead to the patient not showing up for the next session or undermine their willingness to use hypnosis again.]

Step 3: Travelling back

Therapist: So just let that part of you, your unconscious mind, that helps you every day, 24 hours, take you back in Belinda's life to the very *first moment* when she had this dry mouth, this nervousness, this tense feeling, making it difficult to breathe, feeling her heart beat faster, her legs weak, feeling apprehension and worry. Maybe, it's a time in her adult life or in her adolescent life... or as a child or even as a small child... just let the unconscious mind take you back there, as it knows so well how to do... allowing you to get in touch with that which you need to see now, that which you are willing to see now, that which the unconscious mind is willing to show you now. Just signal when it happens.

Patient: *[Nods.]*

[It is of utmost importance that the therapist pronounces the exact words that the patient uses to describe their body feelings and emotions. Watkins proposed these as an "affect bridge" (Watkins, 1971). The affect bridge provides a path to travel within the associated memory. Associated memory links the occurrence of the same body feelings and emotions at different moments in life. It's as if this type of memory provides the necessary information in order to make the best decisions for our protection or success. This affect bridge gives us access to those important and pertinent moments in the patient's life, which are difficult for therapists to identify, even with a great deal of knowledge about the patient.]

Step 4: Observation

Therapist: Very good... and now just take a look around at what's happening to Belinda at that moment, then. When you've seen all that there is to see, you can just let me know.

Patient: *[Nods.]*

Therapist: Now, maybe you could just tell me in a few words what is happening to Belinda, at that moment there, as you continue looking.

Patient: I am 19 and I have had my car crash where I went through the front window. I am badly scarred and it feels as if everybody is telling me that I must learn to drive now. I don't want to. But I start driving lessons. Before I have to go to my lesson I feel so ill. I just can't do it. I just go back to before the car crashed and I go through the window. I'm just so frightened.

I feel stupid because I can't learn to drive. I am embarrassed. My driving teacher is a very nice man and sees that I'm a young girl. He says that it's no good and that I have to stop the lessons. He told me, "You may be able to drive one day but it's definitely not in the near future." It's the same feelings every time I'm going to this lesson; all day I'm dreading it and the people telling me that I have to do it and if I don't it's because it's my fault.

Therapist: So, it's when Belinda is preparing to go to the lesson that she feels bad, because they're making her drive and she doesn't want to.

Patient: Yes, it's too near the accident.

[This phase allows the observing patient to discover the negative life experience linked to her difficulties. The patient's position of observer protects her from the original

full emotional experience and re-traumatization. When describing the cold facts, the patient maintains a comfortable distance from the events.

*The therapist uses certain phrases to reinforce the dissociation. "What is happening to Belinda **there**, at **that moment, then**?" The therapist uses the patient's first name when referring to the regressed younger self. He or she talks with the patient using the pronoun you; for example, "Maybe **you** can just look around to see where Belinda is now and what she's doing."*

The patient is in a central position during communication. The patient speaks directly to the therapist and directly to the younger self. The therapist can only talk to the patient.]

Step 5: Re-parenting

Therapist: So, maybe now you can say hello to Belinda. Maybe she needs somebody to be there with her.

Patient: Oh yes.

Therapist: Just tell her that you're there for her, that you will always be there for her and that she will always be able to feel your presence. And in order to feel that presence, you might want to open your arms and allow her to come into your arms, feel the warmth of your body, and you might want to hug her a little bit, if this is ok for both.

Patient: *[Nods and joins her arms together in front of her.]*

Therapist: How is that going?

Patient: It's going very well.

Therapist: Maybe you can add that you love her with a very special love... an unconditional and everlasting love...

which she will be able to feel at any moment of any day, especially when she needs it. When that's done, just let me know. Take all the time you need, use your own words if needed.

Patient: [Nods.]

Therapist: Okay. Maybe you can look at her face now. How does it look?

Patient: It looks relaxed and she's smiling.

Therapist: That's great.

> [During this phase, the therapist helps to recreate the experience of attachment. When the younger self experiences the patient's physical presence and constant love, it builds inner security.]

Step 6: Evocation and finding a new solution

Therapist: Maybe now you can ask Belinda to tell you in her own words, what's happening there at that moment. You can speak to her, hear her voice, easily. She can do the same for you. It's a very special moment.

Patient: Yes.

Therapist: Okay. When she has told you what she needs to share with you, maybe you can share it with me in a few words.

Patient: She is tired of being pressed. It would be better if people just gave her time.

Therapist: Is there something that she wants to do now to make it better for her?

Patient: She wants to just take [her] time that's all.

Therapist: How can she go about getting this time?

Patient: People are pressuring her. She has to say no—not let people pressure her—nor make her do it and make her feel stupid, or a failure.

Therapist: How can she do that?

Patient: By having more self-confidence and not giving in. By saying, "This is what I want to do, it's not what you want me to do."

Therapist: Okay. How does she sound when she's saying this to you? Does she sound convincing?

Patient: She's quite convincing.

Therapist: Could you ask her to say it in a more convincing voice so that the people could hear what she is saying, maybe she could say it out loud?

Patient: [In a rather determined voice,] I will do what I want to do when I'm ready to do it. I don't need anybody to decide for me, I can decide for myself.

Therapist: How does that sound to you now?

Patient: That sounds more convincing.

Therapist: Do you think she could become even *more* convincing so that she could feel it in every fiber of herself, in her whole body?

Patient: That seems a bit difficult.

Therapist: What would she need to be able to do to accomplish this?

Patient: She would need to have more faith in herself.

Therapist: What's keeping her from that faith?

Patient: Her memories. She seems to be crushed all the time.

[This phase is designed to create and live the positive change, the successful scenario. The younger self acts to accomplish this. If this is impossible the therapist can ask the patient to propose an appropriate action to the younger self. If the younger self is too young to act, the patient might want to protect the younger self by taking him or her from the scene in a reassuring manner. Lastly, the therapist might suggest an action to the patient. In order to be successful, the younger self and the patient must agree on the chosen action.

In our case study, the younger self is somewhat successful in voicing her opinion, but it's not solid enough. Intuitively, I realize that she has not gone far enough back in the past. Maybe there is an earlier problem situation? I suggest that the patient ask the younger self to establish a second target.]

A second step 1: A new target

Therapist: Maybe you can ask Belinda what she is feeling in her body as she feels crushed. Where is she feeling it in her body?

[Patient points to her chest.]

Okay. And what else is she feeling in her body?

Patient: Trembling and weakness.

Therapist: Maybe now you can ask her what emotions she is living with these body sensations.

Patient: [Hesitates...] She feels frightened. She wants to run and hide.

Therapist: Okay. Very good. And now, maybe you can ask her to go back in her life to a moment when she was feeling this crushed feeling in her chest; the trembling, this

weakness, and feeling frightened, a really important moment earlier on.

Patient: Yes.

Therapist: Take a look at this moment and what is going on. Let me know when you have seen all that there is to see.

[Patient nods her head.]

A second step 4: Observation

Therapist: Can you tell me what's happening?

Patient: She doesn't know!

A second step 5: Re-parenting

Therapist: Now maybe you can tell her again that you are there for her and let her feel your warmth—let her know that she will always be able to feel your presence and your unconditional love.

Patient: Yes.

A second step 6: Evocation

Therapist: Maybe you can ask her age?

Patient: Yes, a little girl, three-to-four years old.

Therapist: And ask her what's happening?

Patient: She has the same emotions, the same feelings as when she is older. Fear!

Therapist: What is she afraid of?

Patient: Her mother. It's really bothering her a lot—the feelings of being useless, no good.

Therapist: Okay. Can she tell you what has occurred, what's happening?

Patient: She really doesn't understand. She's with her mother [*Patient now in tears*].

Therapist: What does the mother say to her?

Patient: Mother says to Belinda, "You'll never do anything in life," that she prefers boys, that her eyes are too close to her bladder because she's always crying, that she needs to toughen up, that she was born to be shit upon; and she [*the mother*] swears over and over again.

Therapist: Okay. What can Belinda do with that? It's really difficult for her.

Patient: She is only a child. She can't do much about it and has to put up with it.

Therapist: What could be done for her?

Patient: She needs to realize that she is only a child

Therapist: Can you help her with that? Can you say it to her?

Patient: Yes.

Therapist: Is it normal that her mother asks so much of her as if she were an adult?

   [*By this question, the patient is asked to look at the situation as an experienced adult.*]

Patient: It's not her fault. It's not Belinda that has the problem.

   [*This is an important realization for the patient who has, since a young age, been living with this negative belief of her incompetence.*]

Therapist: Ok. Let her know that.

Patient: Yes.

Therapist: How is she feeling now?

Patient: Better, not yet okay.

Therapist: Could I suggest something to help?

Patient: Yes.

Therapist: Ask her to grow up to your body size of today, in front of her mother. When she has done it, let me know.

Patient: Okay. Yes.

Therapist: As Belinda looks at the situation now, what does she feel that she can do about it?

Patient: Now she can reply. She wasn't hopeless. She has made something of her life and it's her [her mother] who has the problem! Not Belinda. She [her mother] is evil.

Therapist: Let me know when she has been able to tell her mother.

Patient: Yes… she's told her.

Therapist: How does Belinda feel now?

Patient: She feels relieved and free.

Therapist: How does she feel in her body now?

Patient: More relaxed but a little bit of tension left.

Therapist: What does she need to do to release the tension?

Patient: I would like to cuddle her, actually.

Therapist: Yes—cuddle her up so that she can feel what she needs to feel at that age; real, unconditional love. And maybe you can tell her that she is going to grow up and be great in all ways—just tell her—what you want to tell her, so that she knows.

Patient: Yes.

Therapist: How does she feel now?

Patient: She feels better, calmer, at peace, more relaxed.

[The child is too small to act against an adult at this age. In a trance state the brain's creativity is quite exceptional. When the therapist suggests to the younger self to grow to the adult body size, it is easy to do. The child is empowered to see the situation in another light and to act in a more effective manner. Then, the patient's compassion and love for the younger self appears through a loving cuddle, confirming the younger self's actions and thoughts. The last tensions disappear.]

Step 7: Bringing back the resource

Therapist: Now, let her take all those good feelings with her and ask her to grow up to 19 years old. When she's there, let me know.

Patient: *[After some time.]* Yes.

Therapist: How does she look at the situation now?

Patient: It's easier. She needs time to get over the accident. She is in control of her feelings. Inside herself she feels more confident. What's important is to feel at peace within one's self and not to try to please other people all the time.

Therapist: Yes, that sounds much more interesting. And now, what can she say to those people who are telling her that she must drive now?

Patient: She says, "I will do it when I'm ready." She feels confident.

Therapist: Is there something else that you need to share with each other?

Patient: No.

Therapist: Can she take all those good feelings with her and grow up to as big and as old as you are today, passing by all the important moments in her life and letting change what changes? Just let me know when she gets there.

Patient: Yes, I'm there.

[*When the acquired resource is brought back to the age of 19, the patient and therapist witness the application of this new way to act and to think about this situation, which did not have a positive solution only a few minutes earlier. While growing up, the younger self visits other associated moments in the patient's life and can bring about positive changes in these without having to do each one separately, at another moment.*]

Step 8: Integration

Therapist: Now, you can just allow her to integrate within you in a very easy and maybe magical way. When that's done let me know.

Patient: [*Nods her head.*]

[*This fixes the acquisition of the new qualities within the patient of today.*]

Step 9: Post-hypnotic suggestion

Therapist: And just know that these positive changes can continue to evolve in the seconds, the minutes, the hours to come without even doing something but just letting them happen, if it's okay for you.

> [*The days following the session are often punctuated by further changes and realizations. The patient learns that all changes do not need to be accomplished in the therapist's office and that the patient can continue to change and adapt on his/her own.*]

Step 10: Return to the safe place

Therapist: When you're ready, you can go back to your safe place. Take all the time that you need there and come back here when you are ready, by taking a deep breath and opening your eyes, returning in a state that is good for you, perhaps energetic, relaxed, or with a mixture that only you know. When you are ready, maybe we can talk about what has happened.

> [*This return to the safe place with its associated good feelings and security assures that hypnosis can be used in the next session.*]

Step 11: Return to the office and discussion with the patient

> [*The patient comes out of her hypnotic state.*]

Patient: I'm sorry. I got so emotional.

Therapist: Isn't it interesting how emotional things deserve the right emotions?

Patient: I have realized that my problems are linked to my childhood. Since I have had so many problems with my mother and my brother these last times—it has all come back in a crescendo.

Therapist: Yes, of course, and how do you feel now?

Patient: I feel more relaxed and at peace.

Case Summary

The patient originally consulted with me to help her address symptoms linked to a car-driving phobia. However, in this consultation she was able to work on a basic problem in her life; her inability to confront her mother (and any other person in an authoritative parental position in her life—boss, insurance expert, etc.). She succeeded in imposing her own needs and desires. She realized that her mother is incapable of a normal loving and caring relationship with her children. She no longer hopes for motherly love from her mother. She no longer feels ashamed or that she had shortcomings. In our next and last consultation, we again used negative age regression. She was able to see herself alive after her car accident at 19 and capable of living her life as she desired. The phobia symptoms disappeared completely. Since then she has benefitted well from her success.

Conclusion

During our life, we have many accomplishments that create resources and provide us with feelings of success, inner strengths that help us deal with life's challenges in a constantly changing world. But, there are those other moments, traumatic ones. Fortunately, our brains have an automatic defense system that can help counter these traumatic moments. Unfortunately, sometimes these automatic solutions are only partially successful, leaving us with the codified symptoms of mental and psychosomatic illness. These limit our capacity to adapt and to fulfill our needs.

We need an appropriate therapy to finish what the unconscious mind has started. In order to accomplish this, our thoughts, body feelings, and emotions linked to the past traumatic situations must change at the same time, providing new positive thoughts, body feelings, and emotions. Hypnosis, through age regression therapy, provides therapists and their patients with an effective tool for creating and enhancing new resources. The plasticity of our brain registers these positive changes. The old, only partially successful ways become inanimate memories replaced by the new.

References

Watkins, J. G. (1971). The affect bridge: A hypnoanalytic technique. *International Journal of Clinical and Experimental Hypnosis, 19,* 21-27.

Oswald, M. & Schekter, M. (2012). Technique des quatres carrés [Four squares technique]. *Journal CH Hypnosis, 22,* 2/2012. (Also available at www.hypnosesuisse.com in English and in French).

CHAPTER 4

Ego-Strengthening Tools for the Empowerment of Women

Julie H. Linden

Julie H. Linden, clinical psychologist, is a past president of the International Society of Hypnosis (ISH) and the American Society of Clinical Hypnosis (ASCH). Long before integrative medicine was popular, she was integrating hypnosis principles and skills into a wide range of areas. In medical settings, she was an early (1975) pioneer of pediatric hypnotic pain management and facilitation of healing in both acute care (e.g., burn patients, medical procedures, emergency room presentations, and preparation for surgery) and chronic illness care (e.g., kidney dialysis, oncology, cystic fibrosis). In clinical psychology, she has forged the path of the integration of play therapy, trauma recovery, and hypnosis. Julie works with clients of all ages and has contributed to the understanding of hypnotic work in a developmental framework. Her varied interests and writing topics cover a wide range, including: children and adolescents, trauma, hypnotic sandtray therapy, gender-sensitive hypnosis and feminist hypnotherapy, ego state therapy, hypnosis and creativity, hypnosis and the brain-gut connection, education and training in hypnosis, as well as hypnosis and leadership. In 1993 she received a special award from ASCH "For her contributions to the Society in promoting the greater involvement of women in teaching and leadership, and facilitating increased sensitivity to women's issues." She is sometimes called the MsMer of hypnosis. Passionate about hypnosis best describes Julie, as she enthusiastically travels the world, lecturing and training others on the enormous potential for healthy change when hypnosis is incorporated into one's health care practice.

*   *   *

This chapter will look specifically at adult women, their challenges to feeling and behaving empowered, and ways to utilize hypnotic ego-strengthening techniques to foster the development of their empowered voices and beings. Hypnosis has been shown to be a powerful tool for healing. Both physical and psychological wounds respond to hypnosis, and these wounds are influenced by the social context, leading us to consider hypnosis as a biopsychosocial tool.

Attention to the social context in which wounds occur allows for a more integrated approach to healing. For clinicians who work holistically in the psychodynamic inner world of clients, the integration of mind, body, and society is foundational. Social context is multi-factorial and may include culture, group identity, gender, age, political climate, academic environment, neighborhood, and family, among many other social contexts. For example, developmental age is one such social context when we think of the variations that can occur between same chronologically-aged children. Gender is another factor and is defined by social expectations and demands. Women—or the gender-associated roles of being female, since here we are speaking not of the sexual determination of X and Y chromosomes, but rather of the roles that define being female—respond well to hypnotic approaches that consider the relational and the social contexts.

For example, young girls at the age of eight or nine often describe how they feel strong, empowered, and equal to their male peers. They convey this in their classrooms, in sports, and in their play. At the same time, many are keenly aware of the different messages their male counterparts receive. They know that boys are instructed that it is "not manly to cry." Typically, girls are not given that type of message. Girls also know that they may be called a tomboy for enjoying rougher sports—and that this is not meant to be praise.

Learning the meaning of what it is to be an empowered woman is a process of self and societal awareness. The natural caretaking and nurturing qualities associated with what is feminine can become stereotypes for weakness, while the stereotypes of male power, aggression, and hierarchy are poor fits for the collaborative maternal woman. So how does a woman find her path?

During my work with women and hypnosis I developed a model called the 5E's of feminist hypnotherapy because I wanted a way to remind myself of the gender journey for women. I developed a model that encourages rethinking the archetypes and stereotypes that shape us. It was also meant to raise awareness of the unconscious and subtle influences that direct our behavior, especially in mental health care. Its use was contrived to be both diagnostic and prescriptive. In this model, the 5E's stand for Empathy, Ego-strength, Embodiment, Equality, and Empowerment. They serve as a reminder of women's strengths and challenges and are the outline, the backbone, for my hypnotic work. The model can be used with men as well, since feminism, for me, is simply about equality. To quote Caitlin Moran (2011), feminism is "simply the belief that women should be as free as men..." (p. 83).

Briefly, the 5E's model begins with empathy, the chief ingredient in the nurturing abilities we associate with the feminine. Lack of confidence and poor self-esteem, which limit many women, respond to ego-strengthening suggestions. The focus on looks and attractiveness of women requires that they understand their relationship to their body. The procreative creature which menstruates, gets pregnant, and lactates has a complex relationship with the body. It is this embodiment that often influences a woman's sense of equality. Modeling and practicing egalitarian principles help to build esteem, to discover strengths, and to motivate healthy change. Achieving one's full sense of self in the world as an active and actualized contributor to the meaning of one's life requires an embodied empowerment. Empowerment flows from owning one's strengths, wisely utilizing one's empathy, and intentionally directing one's life choices.

So how does this work in hypnotherapy?

Forging identity and finding voice for women means we must first learn what it means to each woman personally to be female. How is she defined? Who defines her? How does she define herself? Women experience confusing and contradictory messages about their personal, social, and professional strengths throughout their growth and development. The societal shaping of gender begins at birth, and family is often the first conveyor of expectations about female behavior. For example, physical prowess is rarely reinforced for girls, while being nice, sweet, and compliant are often reinforced. Whether conscious or unconscious, the messages children receive usually match the stereotypes of their sex; i.e., boys do this and girls do that. One of the first steps in promoting awareness about one's sense of empowerment is to explore the family dynamics, the role models that have been internalized, and the messages that were received from important family members. Hypnotic experiences can facilitate this discovery.

One of the techniques I have found useful to begin the gender journey is rather involved. It is designed to help women explore and discover their identities as women as the first step in finding their strengths and power. I have named this the Identity Portraiture technique. It is also an ego-strengthening technique. Here, I am defining ego-strengthening techniques as those that reinforce healthy efforts, enhance a sense of self efficacy, and facilitate persevering by facing fears in the context of support, learning from mistakes, reframing the negative, evaluating risks to change, developing belief in the ability to succeed, and rehearsing new behaviors.

Begin by guiding the client to a receptive state of trance. For this, many clients have developed their preferred ways of entering this state of mind, so they are invited to use what is familiar and comfortable. Then, utilize the following induction, personalized with words, images, and feelings that mirror and reflect the client.

Transcript

Clinician: This is your time to explore and discover the many components of what it means to you to be a woman. Few of us take the time to ask this question about our identity as female, although we feel instinctively that we know the answer. It is a useful question to ponder. What makes you know you are female? What is important to you about being female? What do you value about your femaleness? And why does this matter?

You are going to enter a space, a place, where you may gather together the people in your life that have influenced your identity as a woman. You may notice that already... images, thoughts, and feelings are presenting themselves to you... just let those images, thoughts, and feelings be there.

[Sometimes images come quickly and unbidden, so preparing the client for this builds trust and a sense that you are present for their journey.]

Take a moment to find the right place for this meeting. Perhaps you will gather these people at a round table. Perhaps you will create a sanctuary and invite them into this sacred space. Or perhaps you will find a place in nature or the universe in which to bring these people together. You may wish to have them standing or seated, near you or at a distance, but configure the setting so it feels just right for you to see and experience their presence. Sometimes, I invite these figures to a picnic outdoors, on a soft comfy quilt, with lots of room for everyone. And sometimes I gather them around a large table, like advisors or personal consultants. I don't know what your place will be, but you will know. ... And you can adjust that place, adding or deleting what is important for you and even changing the setting for one or another figure.

[The place for this gathering is, in itself, significant and personal. Later, you may inquire as to what the place was that came to mind or was created for the gathering. It is important to suggest a structure without too much detail so the client may find what works best for her. Often, clients find the place is an archetype of home, work, or an inner private place. It is also important to provide motivation for this exercise, since the client may at first believe it is obvious

what it means to be a woman and only later realize the complexities of her identity.]

Now, notice the figures you wish to invite into your space and even those that show up unexpectedly. These people may be real or imaginary. They may be from the present, the past, or the future. They may be from your family, ancestors, relatives, friends, or from history, mythology, books, movies, current events, cartoons, or any character that has influenced your identity. They may be female, male, or neutral.

[Again, open-ended, permissive suggestions are important. Naming the many sources for archetypal, stereotypical, and real influences stimulates a deeper exploration of the many influences on identity. If you suggest resources that you know are familiar to your client, this further personalizes the experience. Some figures show up "uninvited," so a suggestion is included for the unexpected. This allows the client to "let happen what happens," providing ample support for unconscious processes and lessening the conscious thoughts that might be over-controlling of the experience. Watch the client during the suggestions of where people may be drawn from, as there is often surprise or recognition on their face, which could prompt a response from you, such as:]

And you may be surprised, pleased, or even angry at who shows up at this gathering. Our identity is forged from so many experiences, some very positive, and some of them may have been experiences that were challenging, unwanted, or even traumatic.

[Because gender identity is developed from a lifetime of experiences, some of which are buried in the unconscious

because they were negative, this suggestion helps to elicit memories and begin a process of reframing those memories.]

Each of these figures that have gathered here have something to give you. You may already know what that gift is, or it may yet be revealed to you. But the gift is one that has contributed to your identity as a woman, and now you have the opportunity to accept or decline the gift. One by one, you will face each of these figures, real and imaginary, in your special gathering place, see what the gift is... and decide if this is *worthy of the woman you wish to be now*. The gift may be in any form. It may be a word or words, an object, an experience, a feeling, a color, any form at all. Begin that process now—one person at a time. See what they have to give you. Decide if you want the gift... or not. One at a time, taking all the time you need in the next few moments to see, listen, feel, and evaluate. ... Is this worthy of the woman you wish to be now...?

[Provide ample time for this experience, and check-in for completion.]

You can let me know when you have considered each of the "gifts" these figures have brought you, simply by nodding your head *[or any ideomotor signal you want to use].*

[Here, it is important to provide stimulus for all and any components of gender identity influences. Keep in mind that there may be universal, archetypal images, so that you may ask questions about those later. The notion that one may assess the "gift" begins the empowering part of the induction.]

Now, take some time to digest and assimilate this experience of your identity as a woman. What has made you the woman you are? How do you define yourself as female, as feminine? Are there elements you wish to change? To discard? To nurture? To strengthen? To celebrate? Make a list of your many strengths, those aspects of your female identity that you enjoy, favor, and wish to maintain. And make another list, of the parts of your female identity that you consider to be liabilities, wish to diminish, or change. Take a picture of each of these lists. Remember them and store these lists in your own special place for future reference.

> [It is important to suggest reflection and memory for this experience, even if it is unconscious memory. Typically, people settle on just a few important items for each list. These become the focus for work on empowerment—on finding their voice and strengthening their identity as women.]

And now, take one of the items from your list of strengths, and imagine a moment in the future where you can see yourself enacting this strength in your actions, words, and/or emotions...

Perhaps you have chosen the strength of speaking your mind and can envision yourself saying what you are thinking to someone important to you... to a partner, a co-worker, or a friend.

Perhaps you have chosen the strength of offering an idea, new and creative, that is different from what another might be offering. See yourself presenting that creative idea, with confidence and ease, secure in your ability to offer a new perspective, a new idea. Choose a strength from your list, and see yourself in a future moment, *being* that strength, *acting* with that strength, *behaving in a way* that exemplifies that strength...

That's right. ... This is you. ... This is the strong female you.

[The examples provided are from my experience of what women cite most often. (Almost always, the woman wants a new way of behaving around men.) Over multiple sessions, each strength can be envisioned and rehearsed in the future. Hypnotic rehearsal of behavior in the future is a form of age progression that reinforces new behaviors. It instills hope and provides practice for reframing. Then you can also take each liability or piece of identity that the woman wants to change, diminish, or discard, and envision a future where that aspect of identity is transformed.]

Again, take a moment to review, reflect, assimilate, and store your experience today. You are discovering and strengthening your inner power, your female energy, the Eve within, the forces of Mother Nature, your voice and your being.

In a moment, it will be time to return to the present, to alert yourself and become aware of your surroundings, back here in…

[Proceed with grounding and alerting suggestions.]

As promised, this technique is complex and layered. It can be broken apart to explore the contributions from one or more of the many sources that contribute to identity, such as family members, workmates, friends, or fiction (among many other sources). The goal is to develop a list of strengths a woman owns in her female identity and those she wishes to transform. In the induction process, leading and pacing her with praise, encouragement, and relational connection through ego-strengthening suggestions is key. This starting place of "Who am I as a woman?" proceeds naturally to empowerment, as new, wished-for behaviors are identified and then rehearsed.

Hypnotic techniques are part of the wider clinical relationship. In my experience, it is most useful for the practitioner to personally experience this technique before using it with someone else. Our hidden biases, assumptions, or self-knowledge about our own identity will be manifested in the relationship. Attention to transference and counter-transference issues is useful. Hypnotic techniques that are incorporated with care, skill, and insight may facilitate rapid change in our clients. Our personal identities are often the focus of clinical work, and to this end, it is hoped you find this Identity Portraiture technique to be productive.

References

Moran, C. (2011). *How to be a woman*. New York, NY: Harper.

For Further Reading ...

Evans, S., & Avis, J. (1999). *The women who broke all the rules: How the choices of a generation changed our lives*. Naperville, IL: Sourcebooks.

Frederick, C., & McNeal, S. (1999). *Inner strengths: Contemporary psychotherapy and hypnosis for ego-strengthening*. Mahwah, NJ: Lawrence Erlbaum.

Gilbert, L., & Scher, M. (1999). *Gender and sex in counseling and psychotherapy*. Boston, MA: Allyn & Bacon.

Hartland, J. (1971). *Medical and dental hypnosis*. London, UK: Balliere Tindall.

Hyde, J.S. (2004). *Half the human experience: The psychology of women*. Boston, MA: Houghton Mifflin.

Linden, J. (1997). On the art of hypnotherapy with women: Journeys to the birthplace of belief and other recipes for life. *Hypnos, 24,* 138-147.

Linden, J. (1999). Discussion of symposium enhancing healing: The contributions of hypnosis to women's health care. *American Journal of Clinical Hypnosis, 42,* 140-145.

Linden, J. (2003). Sandtray hypnosis. *Hypnos, 30,* 196-203.

Linden, J. (2009). Identità di genere: Essere donna oggi [How we define our feminine selves: The kaleidoscopic view of gender identity]. In C. Casula (Ed.), *Le scarpe della principessa [The princess's shoes].* Milan, Italy: FrancoAngeli/Le Comete.

Miller, J. (1986). *Toward a new psychology of women.* Boston, MA: Beacon Press.

Philpot, C., Brooks, G., Lusterman, D., & Nutt, R. (1997). *Bridging separate gender worlds.* Washington, DC: American Psychological Association.

Quindlen, A. (2012). *Lots of candles, plenty of cake.* New York, NY: Random House.

Tannen, D. (1990). *You just don't understand: Women and men in conversation.* New York, NY: William Morrow and Co.

Unger, R. & Crawford, M. (Eds.). (1992). *Women and gender: A feminist psychology.* New York, NY: McGraw Hill.

Zucker, A. (2004). Disavowing social identities: What it means when women say, "I'm not a Feminist, but...". *Psychology of Women Quarterly, 28,* 423-435.

CHAPTER 5

Poetic Language and Hypnosis: The Interplay of Rhythm, Spaces, and Suggestion

George P. Glaser

George P. Glaser, clinical social worker, is a past president of the American Society of Clinical Hypnosis (ASCH), current president of the Central Texas Society of Clinical Hypnosis, and co-founder of the Milton H. Erickson Institute of Austin. He has been involved in leadership and organizational development roles within ASCH since the early 2000s. George has worked in the mental health arena since obtaining his master's degree at The Ohio State University in 1975. His career spans public and private mental health enterprises, spending the last 20 years in his Austin private practice. George's primary clinical interests are with adolescents and adults, with areas of specialization including anxiety disorders, chronic pain, psychosomatic conditions, psychophysiological adjustments to chronic illness, and work with couples. He enjoys helping clients develop a different relationship with their troubles in ways that increase their hope and flexibility.

*   *   *

I have been interested in the relationship of poetic language and rhythm to psychotherapy and clinical hypnosis since the early 1990s. Of the various influences in my 40-plus-year career, this interest is primarily traceable to studies with students of Milton Erickson, most notably Stephen R. Lankton and Stephen Gilligan. I found that when my therapeutic work with a client was "clicking," my language was more rhythmic than my normal speech, and it involved a type of precision that seemed to me quite intriguing. Such carefully constructed language appeared to create conditions for a deeper and more substantive interpersonal connection. The hypnotic effects also seemed more potent. This realization about the interpersonal aspect of the work fits elegantly with the way our field is moving to a greater appreciation of the interpersonal nature of the trance experience.

This discovery about rhythm and pacing led me to pay careful attention to the construction and delivery of my language during therapy, which I eventually came to think of as a poetic form of language in its own right. When I was experientially connected and successfully engaged with a client in some unconscious exploration, it often seemed as if I was composing and speaking a free-verse poem. This in turn led me to pay even more attention to the way I was listening to the client and what I was listening for. I use the term "poetic language" to refer to an oral presentation that purposefully promotes an emotional/unconscious experience. It is admittedly a broad definition, but the more I read and listen to poetry the better it seems to fit me as a therapist.

We all encounter the client who speaks in a way that touches us, while another client, who perhaps has an even more disturbing life story, does not prompt the same emotional response. Is it the story that moves us, or is it a story that is *presented* in a manner that creates greater dramatic tension, or some combination of these? Could it be that the presentation of the words, the rhythm, the refrains, the facial expressions, body movements, or some type of transferential or counter-transferential elements connects us at a deeper emotional and experiential level?

There are distinct differences in the way this free-verse associative process manifests in my work with various clients, which prompted curiosity about where this stuff was coming from. What is the origin? And perhaps most importantly, can the process be duplicated and taught to others?

There are at least two forms of poetic delivery that are relevant here: (1) a straightforward speaking of the poem and (2) an interwoven or embedded format that I illustrate in the induction and deepening with my client "Karen." One might conjure up images of a poetry reading as I write about poetic language in clinical work. While such reading is occasionally applicable, in this chapter I refer to the naturalistic poetic presentations people use when speaking or writing about their lives and the problems for which they seek help. Poetry by nature tends toward metaphorical expression. We know that metaphor is a useful device for describing both problems and transformative processes. Rumi's poem "Guest House" (Barks, 2004) is a marvelous example of a suggestion toward helping us accept unpleasant emotional experiences without unyielding self-judgment.

The essence of this approach is the therapist speaking with emotional precision and power *by utilizing in part the language and imagery of the client*. I'm reminded of a quote by guitarist Ry Cooder, where he mentioned the importance of "not wasting notes" while speaking about using a precise musical style in his performances. I suppose the same can be said for therapeutic language. While working hypnotically in this manner I tend to be talkative, with long pauses to assist with deepening and integration of the therapeutic suggestions.

I recommend two steps for connecting the therapist with the naturalistic poetic language of the client, and these are useable singly or in combination. In one's early use of this approach, singly might be more helpful. First, listen carefully for the natural presentation of the problem or experiential quandary. How does the client present the information to you? Is it presented in a script-like fashion, as if the recitation has been repeatedly practiced, so that little thought, self-awareness, or imagination is required for the "performance" of the story? Or is it a rather disorganized presentation, full of loose ends and hanging threads? Secondly, note any naturalistic refrains that are part of the client's storytelling, especially if they are metaphorical in nature. For example, a divorced woman in her 30s (whose session transcript is presented at the end of this chapter) used the refrain of "No more excuses" when talking about changing her historical and persistent use of wine in the evening to help create a dissociative emotional experience for herself.

Another example of poetic presentation comes from a woman in her 60s who described an almost life-long problem with eczema. She would copiously journal following our sessions, and we developed a routine of her bringing in the previous session's notes, which I would read aloud in a poetic style during the initial part of the session. One specific journal entry was very powerful in presenting the changes she was undergoing, and we entitled it, "Under My Skin." Much of our work was hypnotically grounded, and these readings proved to be excellent deepening and therapeutic experiences for the client. They also helped me understand her in a deeper way.

Consider the client's presentation of the problem as a raw, unfinished draft of a poem. It's as if the patient is trying to compose a story, and they find themselves circling back to the same old ending. This is likely to be a story that has been told repeatedly with only first-order changes. A major part of our therapeutic responsibility and power lies in helping the person change the relationship they have with this stagnant story line.

Listen for the client's refrains. Such repetitive phrases often serve as the title and first line of a useful poem. Most of the time there is no need to formalize a poem, because the story itself is not the driving force, but rather the timing and delivery of the language within a solid and safe therapeutic relationship. A refrain can be about anything meaningful: the presenting problem, a feeling, a longing, a memory, or a question about where to go and how to change the storyline.

It is disappointing for me to hear a poet read their work aloud as if it were a newspaper report. It seems clear in such instances that words alone are not what produce the emotional/unconscious experience in the listener, no matter how well-crafted and incisive. This leads to another question, "What is the relationship between the poet and their audience and how is it affected by the performance?"

The same question can be asked about many elements of psychotherapy. How do we take our scientific knowledge about bodies, psychology, neurology, interpersonal neurology, and behaviors, and artistically use it all to engage the other person in a transformational process? The words of a song may be dazzling, but it is not just the words that produce the emotional response, but rather the relationship between the singer and listener(s) using the experiences of sounds, words, spaces, phrasings, rhythms, and embedded suggestions for the creation of imagery and emotion.

In your practice with this approach, consider disregarding the content of the story and occasionally focusing solely on the rhythms and emotional tone of the story. Think of it as an experiment in listening.

My reasons for employing this approach include:

1. It helps the therapist move into a more intuitive, relational space.

2. It helps the client feel more connected to the therapeutic relationship and process.

3. It increases therapeutic access to the therapist's and client's imagination.

4. It appears to help the therapist and client move into a greater state of unconscious connection that increases the power of the therapeutic interactive field.

How can a therapist introduce these ideas to a patient? How does one start listening for the organic poetry that may be a part of the clinical presentation by the patient? As is true with most things, it becomes easier with practice. For some clinicians, I'm sure my description of the process already seems like second nature. For others the idea may sound strange, this idea of listening for poetry and condensing the client's comment into a poetic format, while purposely seeking to enter a light hypnotic state with the client. Doesn't the therapist have to be alert and in charge of the proceedings?

It may be helpful to consider the processes and performance of a successful athlete. When considering highly active team sports such as football, basketball, and soccer, the necessary state of relaxation involves access to strength, speed, and quickness. These are not qualities we normally consider when thinking about hypnosis or relaxation; however, they are qualities connected with focus, and that is one of the main points under consideration here. The successful athlete has to weave together a relaxed body with a toned and "ready" body. In like fashion, I believe that the therapist must be sharply focused on the client while intensely connected to his or her own experience. The therapist needs to monitor her or his experience, the client's experience, and the interpersonal experiential field.

I have found this approach to be very useful in the development of rapport and increasing a sense of intuitive connection. It is a very interesting and constructive tool for "unconscious tuning," which, when accomplished, makes the entire therapeutic process much smoother. With that in mind, I find it a useful tool in exploring what are the goals for change, and what are the goals of the trance experience.

Below is a transcript of a session with Karen that occurred in June, 2017, with my interspersed commentary. When this session occurred, I had worked with Karen for three years in two separate treatment episodes involving a variety of issues. Her first presenting problem involved significant pain with esophageal spasms, with a history of esophageal surgery at age 22 following a diagnosis of achalasia. This pain responded well to clinical hypnosis, and the improvements in her gastric functioning, including the need for decreased medication levels, have largely maintained to the present.

This 17-minute hypnotic segment illustrates one version of a poetic approach, especially in reference to ways of utilizing the client's language related to desired changes.

Session Transcript:
"Karen with No Excuses: The Last Big Thing"

[Note: Time markers are included in the transcript to provide the reader with a sense of the flow of the session.]

George: So, you said something about when you were telling me about the drinking, that it's "the last thing... the last thing, right?"

> [This statement proposes an idea that can possibly be used as a refrain.]

Karen: Yeah, I feel like it's the last big hurdle...

> ["The last big hurdle" is another possibility for a foundational statement of the poem. Here I attempt to playfully inquire about this phrasing and what it could mean for Karen.]

G: The last big hurdle?

K: Yeah, if I can manage this part of my life I can really open up to my potential.

G: So, the drinking is keeping you from opening up to your potential?

K: I think I hide behind it.

G: You hide behind the drinking? ... You hide behind the wine? [1:00]

> [At this point in the session, I'm starting to see probable spontaneous hypnotic phenomena with increased duration of eye-blinks, with some closures of up to several seconds.]

K: Yes... I think so. [Nods head and closes eyes.]

G: OK. [Long pause.] The last big thing!

K: Yeah.

G: I wonder what it would be like for that last big thing to transform...

[Here we return to the initial "poetic" phrase. My attempt at this point is to interactionally explore with Karen the congruity of this idea among her different "minds." I invite her to imagine a different story.]

K: I think about it all the time... but *[touching her chest]* I get scared... I feel fear, too, when we talk about it.

G: Tell me about it!

K: Um, I fear that, oh it's a... well, I fear failure. First, not being able to control it... uh, and what that means about me, and what that means about my future. Um, I fear life without it. ... I mean it's like a Band-Aid for me. It helps me shut down, relax, turn things off, be a more interesting person, I think, or I have thought in the past. ... I don't think that anymore. Um, because over time the alcohol has started to affect me in a different way. *[2:24]*

[Karen is animated during this part. Here she speaks about her relationship with the wine. I should note that Karen is not a lonely person in the typical sense of the word. She is well liked and has many close girlfriends. She has frequent contact with her divorced mother who lives elsewhere. And yet, it seems like her most enduring relationship is with the alcohol. She speaks here about a developing change in her emotional and physical perspective.]

G: Hmm, How?

K: I feel like just physically affecting me in a different way... like dizzier. It doesn't... it doesn't, it honestly doesn't relax me that much anymore, it causes anxiety. So, I guess I'm having a different chemical reaction to it.

G: You don't feel as good when you drink it as you used to...

K: No, I don't... no, I don't, I really don't... and yet I still can't really seem to give it up. *[3:04]*

[We've reached a point where further conversation is not likely to get us anywhere. Since we have previous experience together in working hypnotically, I simply ask her to focus inside and she readily agrees. I could argue that this is the induction. Here, I combine the refrains of "last hurdle" and "last big thing" as linguistic mechanisms with the intention of focusing her attention internally in a deeper, experiential manner.]

G: So, let me ask you to go inside. *[3:16]*

K: Okay.

[Karen smiles, puts her hands on lap and uncrosses her legs.]

G: And it seems to me that this last hurdle, this last big thing, which may or may not be true. ... I mean it may be your last big hurdle, or it may not be your last big hurdle... your big thing. But as you go inside, let your mind open, to these different possibilities, the possibilities of letting go of this Band-Aid.

Letting go of this crutch, of this thing that is felt needed by you for you to be you. For you to show the world you. Somehow there was the idea that you couldn't be you, couldn't show the world you, without alcohol. Is that correct? *[4:39]*

[In the section above I'm speaking to Karen in a conversational manner. She responds and replies at times with ideomotoric responses indicating agreement with my statements.]

K: *[Shakes head]* Uh hum... I don't think I know who I am without it. I mean I started at 14.

G: And would it be okay to find out who you are without it?

[This question contains an implied suggestion that she "can find out."]

K: It would, but one of the fears I have is that I won't have anything else to blame... like I get rid of that and I can't... I don't have a scapegoat for my behavior.

[In the section above, Karen continues to converse with me in a fairly normal manner even though her eyes are closed.

In the next paragraph, I offer another set of suggestions related to imagining herself and her life in a different way, combined with deepening suggestions. Integrating the stages aspects of inducing trance, deepening trance, and the therapeutic work as separate pieces seems like a sensible and more pragmatic approach than thinking of them in isolation.]

G: Hmm. Well, let yourself imagine life like that. Go deeper inside, and as you go deeper inside, just again, the invitation to let your mind open... your dreams come very vividly, and imagining a life where you did not... where you didn't have an excuse... we could imagine no excuse about this particular topic or we could imagine no excuse period... that Karen lives her life without excuse... that Karen is direct, clear, thoughtful, emotional, intelligent, loving, not loving, giving, selfish. She's all kinds of things... with each breath just go deeper inside. That index finger on your right hand developing that pleasant lightness... it is a good indication of a deepening, a movement into a deeper state of unconscious thought... unconscious experience.

[10-second pause.]

And as you move deeper inside this notion of your mind opening... imagine... imagining Karen with no excuses. I mean I'm not telling you that you should do that by any means, I'm not saying that you should do that, we all have our excuses, but I am asking you to imagine what it would be like to not have any as that finger gets lighter... deeper inside.

[Long pause.]

Lighter and deeper. This mind, this creative mind, the possibility of Karen... no excuses. No excuses! That finger getting lighter and lighter and I wonder when it will want to float entirely off of your leg. Your breath is slow and comfortable. *[9:23]*

> *[Above, I start suggesting to Karen that she go deeper inside by turning to her imagination. She starts to display some finger levitation, and later she starts to demonstrate levitation of the right arm. Her overall appearance suggests a deep state of ease.]*

G: You've learned how to be more comfortable in your body, in your gut... perhaps it's more correct to say that you have learned... you've learned to let yourself *be* comfortable in your gut. But back to this idea of "Karen with no excuses." Now, I would think that Karen with no excuses, my fantasy is *that* Karen would be very powerful. That... that would be a very powerful Karen. My fantasies are both important and a dime a dozen. *[10:49]*

> *[Here, the focus on the body has particular relevance given the overall positive changes in her ability to deal with the original presenting problem of digestive dysrhythmia. We seamlessly move back into the theme of "no excuses." I want to be able to share my fantasies with her... after all, I am also*

in a light trance, but I also don't want to state or imply that my fantasies are too important. I believe the phrasing about fantasies is a helpful way of "playing" with her unconscious mind.]

G: And perhaps your unconscious mind wouldn't mind moving that lightness to the rest of your right hand as well. And developing that buoyancy in the rest of your right hand as you go even deeper inside. That's right! *[This last comment was in response to some more slow, upward hand movement.]* The unconscious mind doesn't always behave in a quick, direct way.

The unconscious mind can meander around to and fro, up and down, back and forth. That hand getting lighter and lighter. Lighter and lighter. Because I think the deeper into trance you go the more vivid can be the fantasy of Karen with no excuses... the woman with no excuses. Deeper and deeper. *[13:02]*

[Weaving deepening suggestions with some mildly confusional statements with the intent of moving Karen back into a state of curiosity regarding a departure from the rationalizations and excuses related to alcohol and her use of it that have been such an important element in her life. Her right hand is almost entirely lifted off her leg and her breathing rate is at 6 cycles/minute.]

The woman with no excuses. I don't know what it's like for you inside, but for me it's a delightful fantasy. I don't know if it's delightful for you, but as that right hand and arm get lighter and lighter I'm inviting Karen's unconscious mind to really have this full-featured, this vivid experience of Karen without excuses... so she can really get a hold of this part of her life, this thing that has been to a certain extent felt out of her grasp. [14:23]

[I use a very playful tone here as I speak about "delightful." Once again, we return to the refrain of "no excuses."]

And wouldn't it be most interesting if your hand began to feel as though it really wanted to touch your face *[long pause]* as your hand and your unconscious mind decide what to do, just, this, this image, this uh scene, this experience of Karen really getting a hold of herself...

[With this language her levitating right hand abruptly turns palm up, as if she was holding something.]

...and going "No more excuses. No more excuses. I'm going to give up that habit. No more excuses." *[Pause]* And when Karen's hand does touch her face, allow a deep sense of knowing to move through her mind and body, a deep sense of clarity to move through her mind and body... a sense of clarity...such clarity that there isn't even any room for excuses. No excuses, they would be, well they wouldn't fit, they would feel out of place... awkward. [17:00]

[Karen's hand continues to move closer to her face, eventually touching it in an apparent state of ease. Here, I continue to use deepening techniques related to focus of attention on the body interspersed with ideas related to the primary poetic elements of the piece—no more excuses. This hypnotic part of the session continues for a couple more minutes.]

This chapter is about a set of ideas and practices I discovered over the course of a long career of trying to figure out practical and potent ways to help people change their minds, bodies, behaviors, and relationships. It presents an approach that can be helpful to any therapist looking for ways to increase their sense of intuitive connectedness with their clients. Being a therapist is a tough job, and any tools we can pick up along the way that make the process more effective, comfortable, and even more pleasurable, are gifts. Using poetry is one of those gifts.

References

Barks, C. (Ed.) (2004). *The essential Rumi: New expanded edition.* New York, NY: HarperCollins.

For Further Reading...

Gainotti, G. (2012). Unconscious processing of emotion and the right hemisphere. *Neuropsychologia, 50,* 205-218.

Iacoboni, M. (2008). *Mirroring people: The new science of how we connect with others.* New York, NY: Farrar, Straus and Giroux.

Marks-Tallow, T. (2012). *Clinical intuition in psychotherapy: The neurobiology of embodied response.* New York, NY: WW Norton.

Oliver, M. (2012). *A thousand mornings.* New York, NY: Penguin.

CHAPTER 6

The Multiple-Embedded Metaphors in Hypnosis

Stephen R. Lankton

Stephen R. Lankton is a licensed clinical social worker (LCSW) in Phoenix, Arizona. He is the editor-in-chief of the American Journal of Clinical Hypnosis *(since 2005) and is a fellow and an approved consultant, American Society of Clinical Hypnosis. He began clinical practice in 1974 and has trained therapists worldwide since 1978. He had the good fortune to have studied for several years with Milton Erickson. He is a diplomate in clinical hypnosis (DAHB), and president emeritus of the American Hypnosis Board for Clinical Social Work. His awards include: the Lifetime Achievement Award for Outstanding Contribution to the Field of Psychotherapy, the Lifetime Achievement Award for Contributions to the Field of Hypnosis and Hypnosis Education, and the Irving Secter Award for the Advancement of Clinical Hypnosis. He is the author/co-author/editor of 18 clinical books and dozens of professional articles and chapters. He studied regularly with Milton H. Erickson from mid-1976 until December 1979.*

*   *   *

The Client

Let's begin by considering the client (modified here to protect privacy). John is a 65-year-old Caucasian male. He was coming to town for a business-related training and wanted to meet with me. I met with him the afternoon before our session so I could obtain a history and have time to plan for our therapy session the following day. He sought treatment to stop his anger outbursts, which could jeopardize his well-being, especially at work. He believes that he explodes, as his parents used to do, when he is interrupted, particularly by individuals who he views as incompetent or less informed than he.

At the time of our meeting, he had been divorced for three years, has no children, and both his father and mother had died within the past four years. He suffered two heart attacks during the stressful time of his mother's death and his divorce. He was a nuclear engineer but changed employment due to his fear of having a third heart attack. His family members were not close; in fact, he, his brother, and his sister seldom speak and when they do it is conflictual and unpleasant. This sibling conflict has existed since childhood. John cannot recall a time after six years of age when his brother spoke to him rather than turning away in disgust for some unknown reason. It appeared to John that his mother favored his sister and severely discounted him and his brother. This dynamic was born out in its final stage when, in her estate, the mother left 80% of her wealth to her daughter and 10% to each son.

A self-reported snapshot of his range of interpersonal behavior shows that his greatest strength lies in a dominant-disaffiliative posture toward others. This is illustrated in the raw score of the Interpersonal Check List (ICL) (Leary, 1957; Lankton & Lankton, 2007/1986; see Figure 6.1).

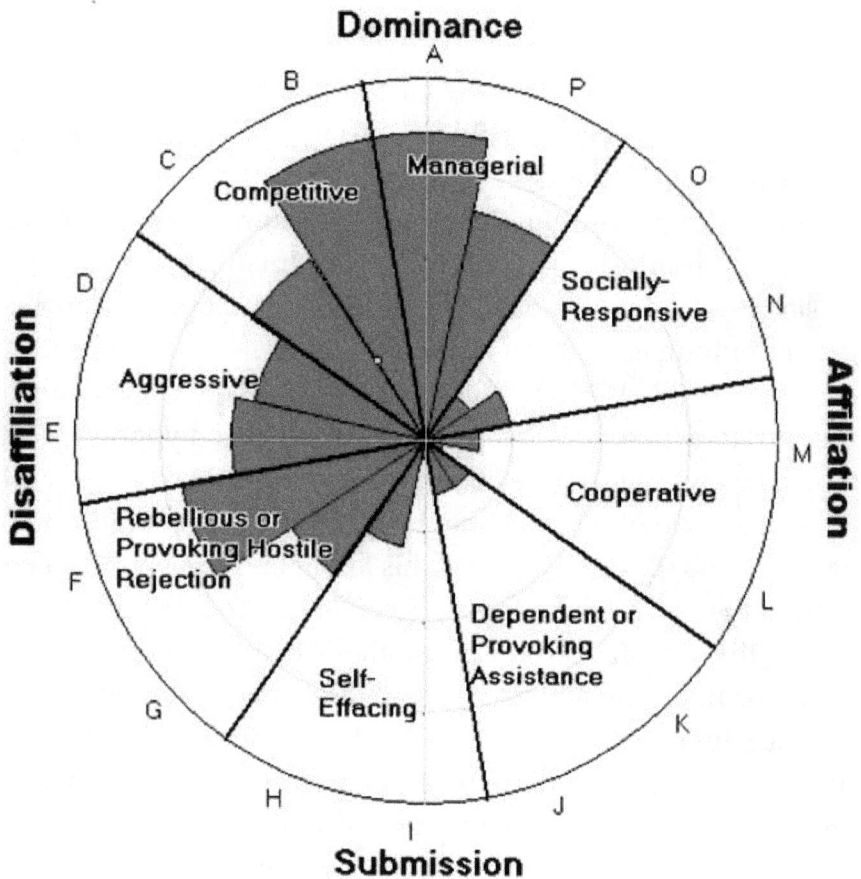

Figure 6.1. The Interpersonal Check List graph for John.

It is apparent and conclusive, from three sources, that he is uncomfortable with the submissive, tender, and weak (certain childlike) aspects of his own personality. To summarize, his family of origin was not accepting of weakness, his self-reported ICL graph shows no submissive behavior, and his presenting problem is that he is often intolerant of interruptions (childlike impulses) and perceived weakness (at least intellectual weakness) in others. At least one major goal of treatment, then, would need to focus on helping him become more accepting of submissive feelings and behaviors in himself and others.

The Session Goals

To address this major concern two goals can be planned. Perhaps the most important would be an emotionally-charged goal to retrieve, accept, and nurture the childlike and weak parts of the self—including creating protection for those parts of the self. However, prior to that self-nurturing goal, it is likely that an attitude-change goal would be useful to challenge the idea that showing weakness is a deficiency and that being strong always pays off.

In addition to these two goals, I planned a metaphor which would serve as an isomorphic overview of his problem and solution. These three goals provide a perfect opportunity to use the Multiple Embedded Metaphors (MEM) framework.

The option to use metaphor as a non-confrontive means to deliver treatment goals seemed particularly appropriate here. Metaphors, or therapeutic stories, as interventions have been associated with the work of Milton H. Erickson for seven decades. His actual use of the term in print was slow to evolve, however. In 1944, Erickson published an article titled, "The Method Employed to Formulate a Complex Story for the Induction of an Experimental Neurosis in a Hypnotic Subject" wherein he demonstrated that a story delivered in trance can have an effect on personality (Erickson, 1944). By 1954, Erickson wrote of using stories which he referred to as "fabricated case histories" to conduct brief therapy (Erickson, 1954, p. 112). Finally, by 1973 Erickson used the term "metaphor" to label a class of his interventions (Erickson & Rossi, 1979, p. 49).

While studying with Erickson durring the last decade of his career, I observed his use of what I termed Multiple

Embedded Metaphors on numerous occasions. That is, Erickson would begin a story that he would then interrupt in the middle by beginning another story. This second story he would again interrupt with yet a third story. Eventually, he would complete the second and then the first stories—usually doing this as a set of three stories. The subjective and observable effect of this technique was notable and appeared to be a common intervention in his work during those years.

Multiple Embedded Metaphors

Beginning in 1983, MEM has been defined and described in several of my publications (Lankton & Lankton, 2008/1983, pp. 245-311). One of my earliest definitions of it is as follows:

> Multiple Embedded Metaphor is a vital tool used to achieve therapeutic goals. The method involves interspersing one metaphor within another, or a number of others, in the course of a single session in order to address certain aspects of three-to-five therapeutic goals. Goals that can be addressed with dramatic therapeutic metaphors include: family structure or development change, age-appropriate intimacy or task behaviors, affect and emotional flexibility, attitude restructuring, self-image thinking, and intensifying discipline and enjoyment (Lankton, 1985, p. 180; Lankton, 2004, p. 176).

A Multiple Embedded Metaphor structure is simply a method of linking several (usually three) metaphors in a manner that amplifies and deepens the effect that would come from the use of a single metaphor (see Figure 6.2). In addition, in contrast to a single goal defined by a single metaphor, the MEM can convey three or more goals, depending upon how it is constructed.

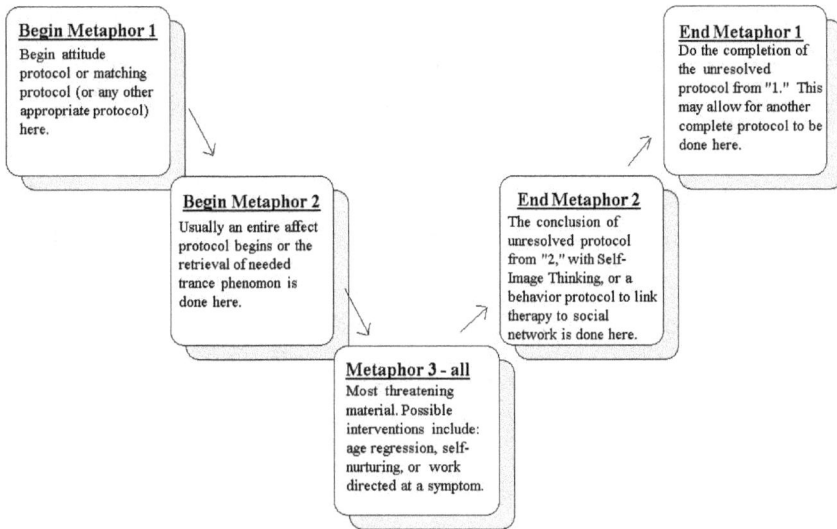

Begin Metaphor 1
Begin attitude protocol or matching protocol (or any other appropriate protocol) here.

Begin Metaphor 2
Usually an entire affect protocol begins or the retrieval of needed trance phenomon is done here.

Metaphor 3 - all
Most threatening material. Possible interventions include: age regression, self-nurturing, or work directed at a symptom.

End Metaphor 2
The conclusion of unresolved protocol from "2," with Self-Image Thinking, or a behavior protocol to link therapy to social network is done here.

End Metaphor 1
Do the completion of the unresolved protocol from "1." This may allow for another complete protocol to be done here.

Figure 6.2. Multiple Embedded Metaphor Structure.

Figure 6.2 depicts the delivery of the content of a MEM. It begins with the metaphor protocol (Metaphor 1) but postpones the conclusion of that metaphor. Instead, another metaphor, with a separate goal is begun at a dramatic point in the first story. This begins Metaphor 2. However, Metaphor 2 is also interrupted with Metaphor 3, often containing the more potentially threatening content. After the completion of the work in the position of Metaphor 3, the conclusion of Metaphor 2 takes place. That is followed by the completion of the goals of Metaphor 1. Due to the embedding of stories, the client's conscious ability to track the logic and flow of some of the material is lost, and the result is often an amnesia for some content in the middle of the structure. That is why Metaphor 3 is best reserved for an intervention that might be the most uncomfortable for the client.

That the delivery of the MEM actually enhances some hypnotic effects like amnesia is supported by empirical research. Mosher and Matthews (1985) investigated the claim that embedding a series of metaphors will create a natural structure for amnesia for material presented in the middle of the metaphoric material. The researchers compared treatment groups who received Multiple Embedded Metaphors with indirect suggestions for amnesia to control groups who received Multiple Embedded Metaphors without indirect suggestions for amnesia. They found support for the structural effect of embedding metaphors on amnesia.

John's Session

Using the above model, let us now look at John's actual session plan. Metaphor 1 was designed as a story of an actor who could play any role except that of being himself. The story is that the actor received an Academy Award for his role as a botanist who helped a misformed tree to become like other trees in the surrounding forest. (The tree had grown too thick in an attempt to protect itself from the harsh environment, one in which other nearby trees did not have to cope.) The story began with his analysis and assessment of the tree's problem but did not continue to the end. It was interrupted by the beginning of Metaphor 2.

Metaphor 2 began an attitude protocol. Specific formulae that maximize a metaphor's likelihood of eliciting desired responses have been elucidated for various goals (Lankton, 1985; Lankton, 2004; Lankton & Lankton, 1989; Lankton & Lankton, 2008/1983). These include, among others, the formulation of attitude challenges which will be used in John's second metaphor and described here. The structure of a metaphor which contains the goal of attitude change can be summarized as follows:

1. Examine the desired attitude, demonstrated by actions of protagonist #1, hinting that it is not desirable.

2. Examine the client's currently held attitude, demonstrated by protagonist #2, hinting that it is desirable.

3. Illustrate these protagonists' different approaches to events in three stages of life—describing a surprise outcome which would be of value to the client and is surprising since it favors protagonist #1's attitude (the desired behavior) and not protagonist #2 (the current attitude of the client).

For the content of this session's attitude metaphor the two protagonists were Barry and Lewis. Lewis's behavior was illustrated as somewhat sensitive. He would tell his teacher when he was hurt or tired or feeling badly. Barry, on the other hand, viewed Lewis's behavior as off-putting and chose to never reveal his hurts, weaknesses, or tender feelings—certainly not in public. The short metaphor depicted the two characters in scenes during kindergarten, high school, and even after employment (as they happened to work in the same company after graduation).

We can deduce from John's history, self-report, and presenting problem, that the most potentially threatening material for him is showing his childlike weakness, fear, and need for comfort. Therefore, this material is addressed in Metaphor 3 as a procedure for self-nurturing. At this time, we ask him to get in touch with this part of himself and also to sense himself as an adult. In this duality, he is coached in listening to, praising, nurturing, and vowing to protect his younger self. He is asked to "trade resources" between these parts of himself. That is, when the weaker part needs comfort he will provide it and when the grown-up part needs tenderness and empathy, the younger part will provide that.

Readers may wonder why this intervention is considered a metaphor. The answer is, it is not a metaphor, as are the others, about third-party characters—it is about John directly. It is direct work on his emotional situation. However, while it could have been done metaphorically, it was done experientially and was embedded within the metaphor framework. For that reason, it is still considered a part of the Multiple Embedded Metaphor framework.

Following the completion of this imagined self-nurturing experience, Metaphor 2 continues. In the conclusion of the story of Barry and Lewis there is an annual meeting of the company in which they both work. An award is presented to the director of the most creative and enterprising department. Barry naturally believes it will be his as he has been a strong and decisive leader. So Barry is completely confused when the award is given to Lewis. Lewis's vulnerability has resulted in his team's greater cohesion and achievement. The moral of the story is not stated for John. Rather, the metaphor was told in such a manner as to engage John's assumption and prediction that Barry (like him) would win with his attitude and approach. But instead, John will have to ponder the outcome and rethink his prediction that strength accomplishes the most.

The end of Metaphor 1 follows immediately. The botanist, who never really understood the reason for the healing, cured the tree by trimming off the excess layers of protective growth and wrapping the tree in gauze. Within a year the tree was healed and was nearly indistinguishable from others. For portraying the role as botanist, the actor received an Academy Award. But the metaphor concludes that the actor never understood what the botanist learned: it is the change that matters, not the understanding.

Figure 6.3 shows what this MEM looked like in my notes. Be aware that the content in the figure represents the key points that would be used to construct smooth stories; I elaborate on these as I construct and tell the metaphor.

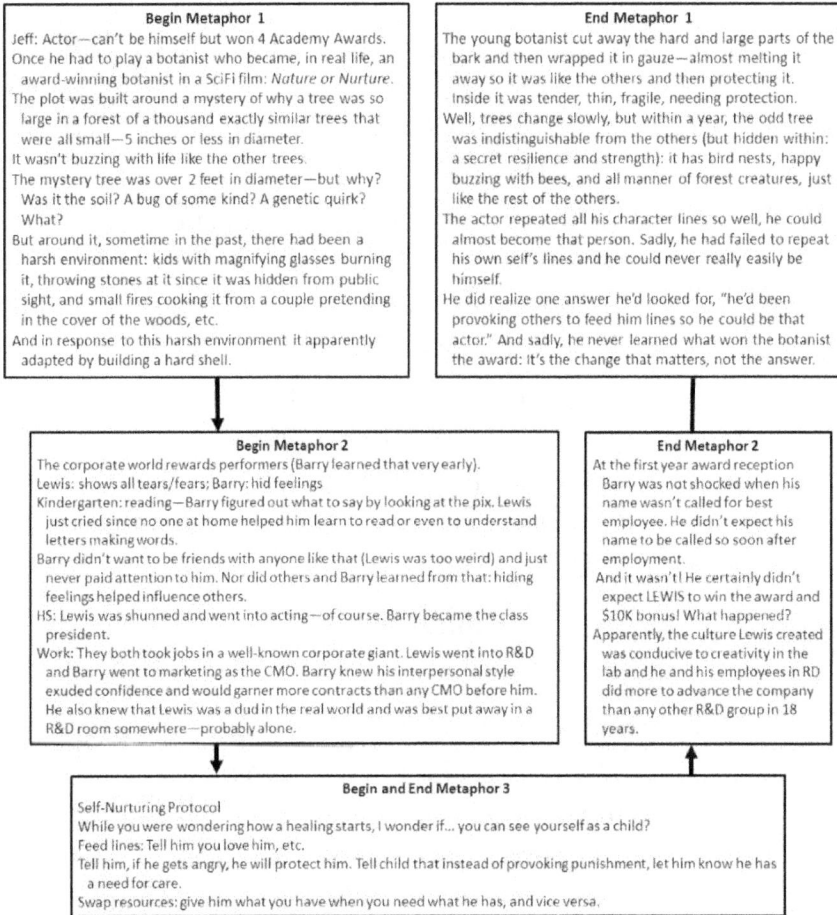

Begin Metaphor 1	End Metaphor 1
Jeff: Actor—can't be himself but won 4 Academy Awards. Once he had to play a botanist who became, in real life, an award-winning botanist in a SciFi film: *Nature or Nurture*. The plot was built around a mystery of why a tree was so large in a forest of a thousand exactly similar trees that were all small—5 inches or less in diameter. It wasn't buzzing with life like the other trees. The mystery tree was over 2 feet in diameter—but why? Was it the soil? A bug of some kind? A genetic quirk? What? But around it, sometime in the past, there had been a harsh environment: kids with magnifying glasses burning it, throwing stones at it since it was hidden from public sight, and small fires cooking it from a couple pretending in the cover of the woods, etc. And in response to this harsh environment it apparently adapted by building a hard shell.	The young botanist cut away the hard and large parts of the bark and then wrapped it in gauze—almost melting it away so it was like the others and then protecting it. Inside it was tender, thin, fragile, needing protection. Well, trees change slowly, but within a year, the odd tree was indistinguishable from the others (but hidden within: a secret resilience and strength): it has bird nests, happy buzzing with bees, and all manner of forest creatures, just like the rest of the others. The actor repeated all his character lines so well, he could almost become that person. Sadly, he had failed to repeat his own self's lines and he could never really easily be himself. He did realize one answer he'd looked for, "he'd been provoking others to feed him lines so he could be that actor." And sadly, he never learned what won the botanist the award: It's the change that matters, not the answer.

Begin Metaphor 2	End Metaphor 2
The corporate world rewards performers (Barry learned that very early). Lewis: shows all tears/fears; Barry: hid feelings Kindergarten: reading—Barry figured out what to say by looking at the pix. Lewis just cried since no one at home helped him learn to read or even to understand letters making words. Barry didn't want to be friends with anyone like that (Lewis was too weird) and just never paid attention to him. Nor did others and Barry learned from that: hiding feelings helped influence others. HS: Lewis was shunned and went into acting—of course. Barry became the class president. Work: They both took jobs in a well-known corporate giant. Lewis went into R&D and Barry went to marketing as the CMO. Barry knew his interpersonal style exuded confidence and would garner more contracts than any CMO before him. He also knew that Lewis was a dud in the real world and was best put away in a R&D room somewhere—probably alone.	At the first year award reception Barry was not shocked when his name wasn't called for best employee. He didn't expect his name to be called so soon after employment. And it wasn't! He certainly didn't expect LEWIS to win the award and $10K bonus! What happened? Apparently, the culture Lewis created was conducive to creativity in the lab and he and his employees in RD did more to advance the company than any other R&D group in 18 years.

Begin and End Metaphor 3
Self-Nurturing Protocol While you were wondering how a healing starts, I wonder if... you can see yourself as a child? Feed lines: Tell him you love him, etc. Tell him, if he gets angry, he will protect him. Tell child that instead of provoking punishment, let him know he has a need for care. Swap resources: give him what you have when you need what he has, and vice versa.

Figure 6.3. The actual session plan and MEM for John.

Summary

John stopped by my office to see me before he left town at the end of the week, following that session. He reported that he had not had any sense of irritation with others at the training (as he had the day before I met with him), and he actually had become friends with the women who had most agitated him. He reported that he received phone calls from work asking him such things as to be on a team with the individual toward whom he had previously had the outburst, and he found himself accepting the invitation without hesitation or tension. He believed that the issue that brought him to therapy was resolved—at least for now. He was, needless to say, very pleased as it meant to him that his stress would be reduced and neither his job nor his health would be threatened by further outbursts.

John's case appears to be a single-session success. However, that outcome, while possible, is not typical. John is a very resourceful and well-educated man and those factors, as well as his motivation, certainly account for much of his rapid success.

Conclusion

Therapy needs to address many facets of a person's or family's interaction with others and with their environment. The multiple Embedded Metaphor is a single, yet powerful, tool for helping in that pursuit. This chapter has outlined the logic and method for constructing Multiple Embedded Metaphors. Further skill in formulating simple metaphors (Gordon, 1978; Lankton, 2003/1980), constructing goal-directed metaphors (Lankton & Lankton, 1989), therapy planning, and supervised training in the clinical use of hypnosis will serve to enhance the ability to employ MEM appropriately and effectively.

References

Erickson, M. H. (1944). The method employed to formulate a complex story for the induction of the experimental neurosis in a hypnotic subject. *The Journal of General Psychology, 31*, 67-84.

Erickson, M. H. (1954). Special techniques of brief hypnotherapy. *Journal of Clinical and Experimental Hypnosis, 2*, 109-129.

Erickson, M. H., & Rossi, E. L. (1979). *Hypnotherapy*. New York, NY: Irvington Publishers.

Gordon, D. (1978) *Therapeutic metaphors*. Cupertino, California: Meta Publications.

Lankton, S. R. (1985). Multiple embedded metaphor and diagnosis. In Jeffrey K. Zeig (Ed.), *Ericksonian psychotherapy, volume 1: Structures* (pp. 171-195). New York, NY: Brunner/Mazel Publishers.

Lankton, S. R. (2004). *Assembling Ericksonian therapy: The collected papers of Stephen Lankton*. Phoenix, AZ: Zeig-Tucker.

Lankton, S. R. (2003/1980). *Practical magic: A translation of basic neuro linguistic programming into clinical psychotherapy* (Rev. ed.). Williston, VT: Crown House.

Lankton, C. H., & Lankton, S. R. (1989). *Tales of enchantment*. Levittonwn, PA: Taylor & Francis/Brunner-Routledge.

Lankton, S. R. & Lankton, C. H. (2007/1986). *Enchantment and intervention in family therapy: A training seminar on Ericksonian approaches*. New York, NY: Brunner/Mazel.

Lankton, S. R. & Lankton, C. H. (2008/1983). The multiple-embedded metaphor framework: The interpersonal framework. In Stephen R. Lankton and Carol H. Lankton, *The answer within: A clinical framework of Ericksonian hypnotherapy* (pp. 141-147). New York, NY: Brunner/Mazel.

Leary, T. (1957). *Interpersonal diagnosis of personality: A functional theory and methodology for personality evaluation.* New York, NY: The Ronald Press.

Mosher, D., & Matthews, W. (1985, August). *Multiple embedded metaphor and structured amnesia.* Paper presented at the 93rd Annual Convention of the American Psychological Association, San Diego, CA.

CHAPTER 7

A Common Factors
Approach to Hypnosis

Guy H. Montgomery

Guy H. Montgomery is an associate professor and director of the Center for Behavioral Oncology at the Icahn School of Medicine at Mount Sinai in New York, New York, USA, and is a licensed clinical psychologist. He is internationally recognized for his research on the use of hypnosis to prevent and control symptoms and side effects associated with cancer and its treatment. His research has been funded by the National Institutes of Health and the American Cancer Society. He has published over 100 empirical articles, has an ongoing National Cancer Institute supported program to train health care providers in providing hypnosis and cognitive behavioral therapy to cancer patients. He has co-edited a book on evaluating the effectiveness of psychotherapies: Evidence-Based Psychotherapy: The State of the Science and Practice *(David et al., 2018). Dr. Montgomery's work in hypnosis has been recognized through awards that he has received, including the Distinguished Contributions to Scientific Hypnosis and Professional Hypnosis Awards from the American Psychological Association's Society of Psychological Hypnosis. For over 20 years, Dr. Montgomery has worked clinically with cancer patients to help them improve their quality of life, and he continues to be an active clinician in his role as director of psychological services at Mount Sinai's Dubin Breast Center.*

*   *   *

I'll admit that I struggled quite a bit in writing this chapter. Like many of my esteemed co-authors, I've been using hypnosis for so long that many aspects feel nearly automatic to me. If I did not firmly support sociocognitive explanations of hypnosis (Kirsch, 1990), I would almost say that I drift into a trance! Kidding aside, nearly as soon as I begin providing hypnosis, as I begin delivering a hypnotic induction, I find myself just slipping into what I call "hypnotic mode." In writing this chapter, I attempted to deconstruct my hypnotic mode, operationalize my process, and articulate it (hopefully clearly) to you, the reader.

Like many of us, my approach to hypnosis was shaped by the supervision and mentoring I received in graduate school. I received my PhD in clinical psychology from the University of Connecticut, under the mentorship of Dr. Irving Kirsch. I originally joined his research team to investigate the psychological mechanisms underlying placebo effects. I was, and still am, fascinated that by simply *believing* that we will feel or react in a certain way, we *create* that experience.

The power of placebo effects to shape patient experiences is quite amazing (Beecher, 1955); however, the clinical application of placebo treatments and interventions are generally limited, due to the element of patient deception. So how can we provide patients with the clinical benefits of placebo while being truthful and straightforward? As Dr. Kirsch recognized, hypnosis fits the bill. Research indicates that placebo effects, at least in part, are due to the effects of response expectancies (Kirsch & Montgomery 1998; Montgomery & Kirsch, 1996, 1997; Price et al., 1999). The effects of hypnosis, at least in part, have also been shown to be due to response expectancies (Kirsch, 1999; Montgomery et al., 2010). Through our induction procedures, suggestions, and even the use of the word "hypnosis" (Gandhi & Oakley, 2005; Schnur et al., 2008; Schoenberger et al., 1997), we can help patients expect to feel better, and through that expectation, they will. That is, hypnosis can be viewed as an ethical and non-deceptive intervention to alter patient response expectancies to increase patient well-being.

My initial appreciation of the power of response expectancy effects opened the door to a broader appreciation for the role of other psychotherapeutic common factors, such as treatment expectations, developing a strong therapeutic alliance, and being empathic (Constantino et al., 2011; Wampold, 2015). Given that I view hypnosis as a psychotherapeutic technique, I reasoned that factors that research has shown to enhance psychotherapy outcomes in general would also enhance hypnosis outcomes. Therefore, my approach to hypnosis focuses largely on enhancing these common factors. I typically head into patient sessions with a basic hypnosis script in mind, but I am of the firm belief that even the most eloquent, carefully worded, beautiful script will fail if the patient does not expect it to succeed, feel comfortable in the therapeutic relationship, or feel deeply and genuinely understood by their therapist. Below, I'll review each common factor and discuss how I work to maximize each when conducting hypnosis sessions.

Alliance

Therapeutic alliance has been defined as consisting of three components: bond, agreement on therapy goals, and agreement on the therapeutic tasks required to achieve those goals (Bordin, 1976).

In any hypnosis session, I begin by developing a therapeutic bond. This work begins right from the very moment I greet patients, when I make sure to verbally and non-verbally convey warmth, caring, and genuine pleasure in the patient's bravery in seeking help and in my ability to be able to offer my services to try to improve their quality of life.

For many patients, participating in hypnosis requires a great degree of trust, even more so than participating in other psychotherapeutic techniques. In recognition of the leap of faith many patients make when participating in hypnosis sessions, I work hard to let them know that I'm an expert, a guide, and a companion in the process; not someone trying to take control of them, to embarrass them in any way, or to dictate their experience.

Throughout the hypnosis session, I strive to be real and genuine; compassionate and reassuring when called for; but also not afraid to be a little goofy or silly, to make a joke at my own expense, or to laugh at common misconceptions about hypnosis. Hypnosis is a serious and efficacious intervention (Montgomery et al., 2000; Montgomery et al., 2002; Schnur et al., 2008), but there's no reason it cannot also be fun! Of course, as in any psychotherapeutic situation, humor needs to be used with caution; but some humor in this circumstance can go a long way to putting a patient at ease and furthering your therapeutic bond.

During the induction, I always emphasize that it is "*Safe* to enter hypnosis now." I let them know that they will experience "Their own experiences, just their own experiences," in order to reduce fears that they will somehow not be in control. I keep my voice "hypnotic" but also warm. I match the pace of my delivery to the patient's breathing and then work to slow the breathing down. I often direct their breathing to encourage patients to take longer, deeper, and slower breaths. Overall, I am trying to meet the patient where they are and guide them to an easy and relaxing hypnotic experience.

Agreement on Hypnosis Goals

Negotiating and agreeing on the goals of a hypnosis session is absolutely critical in shaping the language to be used. Generally speaking, unless a patient has extremely high levels of hypnotic responsiveness, I consider hypnosis to be a tool to reduce symptom intensity and associated bother, rather than a magic wand to make all aversive symptoms simply disappear (although I sometimes wish it could). Therefore, my goal is to help reduce the patient's symptoms.

Yet many patients enter hypnosis with a different goal; that of completely eliminating a bothersome (sometimes chronic) symptom, ridding themselves of a long-term habit in one session with no follow-up work or effort, or radically changing their personality. In essence, many patients may anticipate a magical cure. An important part of providing hypnosis interventions is finding a way to meet in the middle in regard to treatment goals. What I mean by that is both (1) maintaining positive beliefs and expectations about the efficacy of hypnosis, while also (2) educating patients about realistic (and still impressive) clinical effects. Prior to the formal induction, I might say something like:

I understand that you are having a lot of pain right now and that you wish that I could just make it all disappear. I wish that too, but let me tell you how patients often respond. Typical patient benefit is gradual, and also increasing. That is, you should begin to feel some relief today, and more and more over time.

Within the formal induction, I might say:

You are going to experience benefit from hypnosis. You might notice a little at first, but like a snowball rolling down a hill, your benefit can gradually increase the further along you go.

Although agreement on goals is critical in any hypnosis session, I find it to be particularly critical in my work with individuals with cancer. I deeply wish that I could make it so that no one undergoing chemotherapy would lose their hair, no one undergoing radiotherapy would feel any fatigue, and that no survivor taking adjuvant hormonal therapies would have any hot flashes or musculoskeletal pain. But I can't. What I can do for the vast majority of patients is help them adjust to hair loss, reduce the severity and bother of fatigue, and reduce pain intensity and hot flash frequency.

Agreement on Hypnosis Tasks

Once we agree on the treatment goals, we also need to agree on what tasks need to be completed during hypnosis in order to achieve those goals. There are a few important aspects to be noted here. First, many patients come in with assumptions about hypnosis. Patients believe that there are certain things they need to do during hypnosis in order to experience benefit. For example, patients may believe that they *must* be able to relax, to clear their mind, to totally "let themselves go," or to be hyper-focused on my words, to name a few. Engaging in these tasks may facilitate hypnotic responding, but they are not necessary. For example, hypnotic inductions have even been successfully conducted while participants were riding on exercise bikes (Banyai & Hilgard, 1976)! Therefore, in the inductions I use, I focus on encouraging patients to be open to the experience, to engage in the process, to listen, and to be receptive to the suggestions.

I don't want patients to feel like they are failing tasks that are not completely necessary in the first place. So, for example I might say:

Just close your eyes and listen to the sound of my voice. That is all you really need to do. You might find yourself beginning to relax while being focused. You might find yourself drifting just a little, and that is perfectly fine. There is no right or wrong. You don't have to be or do anything. Just follow along with the sound of my voice.

However, there is one task that I do strongly recommend. Like any other type of psychotherapy, I view hypnosis as an intervention technique that improves with a patient's practice, input, and commitment. For many, hypnosis is a skill, like riding a bike; the more the patients practice the more quickly and easily they will be able to achieve hypnotic benefit. So, during the hypnosis session I'll suggest that:

As you continue to practice hypnosis, you might find that it becomes easier and easier. Easier and easier to relax, easier and easier to follow along, and easier and easier to feel better.

Empathy

Carl Rogers defined empathy as, "The therapist's sensitive ability and willingness to understand the client's thoughts, feelings, and struggles from the client's point of view. [It is] this ability to see completely through the client's eyes, to adopt [their] frame of reference..." (Rogers, 1980, p. 85).

Based on work by Barrett-Lennard (1981), I consider empathy in the context of a hypnotic intervention to have three main phases: (1) the hypnotist has empathic resonation with the client, (2) the hypnotist works to convey their understanding to the client, and (3) the client receives this communication. In a hypnotic intervention, I find empathy to be a key construct, not only in terms of helping the client feel safe, heard, and respected, but also in shaping the language of the induction and suggestions.

When a patient describes a symptom, I work to empathically imagine and understand their suffering, to convey my best understanding of their experience to them, and to check in with the patient to see if my expression of understanding feels right to them. So, in my discussions with the patient I may come to understand that their fatigue feels like physically being "crushed" or like "running into a brick wall" or like "fighting my way through Jell-O"; their pain may feel like "fireworks going off," or their neuropathy might feel like "pebbles in my toes." In the induction and suggestions, I make sure to use the patient's language to ensure that they feel understood. So instead of saying, "You feel less and less fatigued," I might say:

You can feel light and free, nothing is holding you back or can get in your way, everything is smooth and easy. The Jell-O is gone, the "crush" is lifted.

Response Expectancies

Response expectancies have been defined as anticipations of one's own nonvolitional reactions to situations and behaviors (Kirsch, 1999; Montgomery & Bovbjerg, 2003). For example, expecting to feel anxious can often lead one to feel anxious (Montgomery et al., 2002). Kirsch (1985) was perhaps the first to explicitly theorize on relations between what individuals expect and their experiences of seemingly automatic responses. He termed such beliefs concerning nonvolitional outcomes, "response expectancies" and explicitly hypothesized that response expectancies are:

sufficient to cause nonvolitional outcomes, not mediated by other psychological variables, and self-confirming while seemingly automatic.

Consistent with Kirsch's theories, the research literature has supported the hypothesis that response expectancies can mediate the effects of hypnosis in health care settings (Montgomery et al., 2010). During hypnotic inductions, I remain aware of how I am setting expectations for nonvolitional outcomes (e.g., pain, fatigue, anxiety). I work to set positive expectations that a patient's symptoms will decrease and that they will feel better and better over time, but I do not oversell. I do not wish my patients to have disconfirming experiences. For example, I might phrase a suggestion as follows:

You might find that you already feel more relaxed and slightly less anxious. Your anxiety is slowly, gradually, and steadily decreasing. Less and less anxious, more and more relaxed. More and more at ease. ... I wonder how far you can go in letting go of your anxiety.

Treatment Expectancies

Treatment expectancies are patients' prognostic beliefs about participating in a treatment (Constantino et al., 2011). These expectancies can change throughout the course of the treatment. That is, patients can come to a treatment session with a set of treatment expectancies, which can change as the patient engages in the treatment. The credibility of a treatment and the treatment rationale can both contribute to overall treatment outcome expectancies. In the case of a hypnotic induction, many patients are new to the experience.

Patients do not know what exactly to expect, but they often hold beliefs about what hypnosis is. Some of these can be positive (e.g., relaxing, powerful, deep), some may be negative (e.g., frightening, embarrassing), some may be realistic (e.g., efficacious, time limited), and some may be unrealistic (e.g., magical, controlling). The clinician who cultivates positive and realistic treatment expectancies will enhance the therapeutic benefit of the induction. Letting patients know that hypnosis is clinically efficacious based on the literature, that hypnosis often has greater clinical benefits than similar mind-body interventions (e.g., relaxation, guided imagery), and that hypnosis can be effective in as little as 15 minutes (Montgomery et al., 2007), all contributes to positive treatment expectancies.

Conclusion

In conclusion, I believe that the benefits of hypnotic interventions can be enhanced through awareness of the role of common psychotherapeutic factors. In the case of hypnosis, some factors, like expectancy, may be part and parcel to underlying psychological mechanisms of hypnosis. Other factors, like alliance, may be especially relevant in order to help your clients feel safe and secure during hypnotic interventions. Overall, this recipe is likely to improve your clinical outcomes, slowly at first, but with greater gains as you continue to practice and employ the technique.

Acknowledgements

I would like to thank Dr. Julie B. Schnur for her contributions in preparing this manuscript.

References

Banyai, E. I., & Hilgard, E. R. (1976). A comparison of active-alert hypnotic induction with traditional relaxation induction. *Journal of Abnormal Psychology, 85,* 218-224.

Barrett-Lennard, G. T. (1981). The empathy cycle: Refinement of a nuclear concept. *Journal of Counseling Psychology, 28,* 10.

Beecher, H. K. (1955). The powerful placebo. *Journal of the American Medical Association, 159,* 1602-1606.

Bordin, E. S. (1976). The generalizability of the psychoanalytic concept of the working alliance. *Psychotherapy: Theory, Research and Practice, 16,* 252-260.

Constantino, M. J., Arnkoff, D. B., Glass, C. R., Ametrano, R. M., & Smith, J. Z. (2011). Expectations. *Journal of Clinical Psychology, 67,* 184-192.

Gandhi, B., & Oakley, D. A. (2005). Does 'hypnosis' by any other name smell as sweet? The efficacy of 'hypnotic' inductions depends on the label 'hypnosis'. *Consciousness and Cognition, 14,* 304-315.

Kirsch, I. (1985). Response expectancy as a determinant of experience and behavior. *American Psychologist, 40,* 1189-1202.

Kirsch, I. (1990). *Changing expectations: A key to effective psychotherapy.* Pacific Grove, CA: Brooks/Cole.

Kirsch, I. (1999). *How expectancies shape experience* (1st ed.). Washington, DC: American Psychological Association.

Kirsch, I., & Montgomery, G. H. (1998). Conditioned enhancement of the placebo response: Expectancy or verbal stimulus substitution? *Pain, 76,* 269-270.

Montgomery, G. H., & Bovbjerg, D. H. (2003). Expectations of chemotherapy-related nausea: Emotional and experiential predictors. *Annals of Behavioral Medicine, 25,* 48-54.

Montgomery, G. H., Bovbjerg, D. H., Schnur, J. B., David, D., Goldfarb, A., Weltz, C. R., . . . Silverstein, J. H. (2007). A randomized clinical trial of a brief hypnosis intervention to control side effects in breast surgery patients. *Journal of the National Cancer Institute, 99*, 1304-1312.

Montgomery, G. H., David, D., Winkel, G., Silverstein, J. H., & Bovbjerg, D. H. (2002). The effectiveness of adjunctive hypnosis with surgical patients: A meta-analysis. *Anesthesia & Analgesia, 94*, 1639-1645.

Montgomery, G. H., DuHamel, K. N., & Redd, W. H. (2000). A meta-analysis of hypnotically induced analgesia: How effective is hypnosis? *International Journal of Clinical and Experimental Hypnosis, 48*, 138-153.

Montgomery, G. H., Hallquist, M. N., Schnur, J. B., David, D., Silverstein, J. H., & Bovbjerg, D. H. (2010). Mediators of a brief hypnosis intervention to control side effects in breast surgery patients: Response expectancies and emotional distress. *Journal of Consulting and Clinical Psychology, 78*, 80-88.

Montgomery, G. H., & Kirsch, I. (1996). Mechanisms of placebo pain reduction: An empirical investigation. *Psychological Science, 7*, 174-176.

Montgomery, G. H., & Kirsch, I. (1997). Classical conditioning and the placebo effect. *Pain, 72*, 107-113.

Montgomery, G. H., Weltz, C. R., Seltz, M., & Bovbjerg, D. H. (2002). Brief presurgery hypnosis reduces distress and pain in excisional breast biopsy patients. *International Journal of Clinical and Experimental Hypnosis, 50*, 17-32.

Price, D. D., Milling, L. S., Kirsch, I., Duff, A., Montgomery, G. H., & Nicholls, S. S. (1999). An analysis of factors that contribute to the magnitude of placebo analgesia in an experimental paradigm. *Pain, 83*, 147-156.

Rogers, C. R. (1980). *A way of being.* Boston, MA: Houghton Mifflin.

Schnur, J. B., Kafer, I., Marcus, C., & Montgomery, G. H. (2008). Hypnosis to manage distress related to medical procedures: A meta-analysis. *Contemporary Hypnosis, 25,* 114-128.

Schoenberger, N. E., Kirsch, I., Gearan, P., Montgomery, G. H., & Pastyrnak, S. L. (1997). Hypnotic enhancement of a cognitive behavioral treatment for public speaking anxiety. *Behavior Therapy, 28,* 127-140.

Wampold, B. E. (2015). How important are the common factors in psychotherapy? An update. *World Psychiatry, 14,* 270-277.

CHAPTER 8

Utilizing, Reframing, and Expanding Patients' Metaphors

Consuelo Casula

Consuelo C. Casula is a graduate in philosophy, having specialized in psychology and clinical hypnosis, and is a Neuro Linguistic Programing trainer, residing in Milan, Italy. She teaches hypnosis at the Scuola Italiana di Ipnosi e Psicoterapia Ericksoniana and at other Italian and international schools of psychotherapy and clinical hypnosis. She is on the Board of Directors of The Italian Society of Hypnosis, the immediate past-president of the European Society of Hypnosis (ESH), and served on the Board of Directors of the International Society of Hypnosis (ISH) from 2009 to 2018. She travels nationally and internationally as an invited speaker to lecture and give workshops at ESH, ISH, the American Society of Clinical Hypnosis, and at Milton H. Erickson Foundation congresses. Recent destinations, for example, have been Japan, Mexico, Brazil, Iran, and China. In her practice she integrates clinical hypnosis with pragmatic, systemic, and strategic approaches, combined with positive psychology and mindfulness techniques. She has published a number of articles as well as eight books on communication skills, leading groups, metaphors, women's development, resilience, hypnotic strategies, and meditation. Her book on metaphors—Giardinieri, principesse, porcospini, metafore per l'evoluzione personale e professionale *(Casula, 2002)*—has been translated into Spanish, Portuguese, French, and German. Her book on resilience—La forza della vulnerabilità: Utilizzare la resilienza per superare le avversità *(Casula, 2011)*—is also available in French. In 2016, she received the IV International Franco Granone Award from the Franco Granone - Centro Italiano Ipnosi Clinica e Sperimentale in Turin, Italy.

*   *   *

The aim of this chapter is to show strategic ways to utilize metaphors as a healing method in therapy (Close, 1998; Hammond, 1990; Siegelman, 1990). I use the word *metaphor* in its multiple therapeutic implications; that is, partly as analogy or therapeutic story, but mainly as guided imagery based on the amplification of the metaphor used spontaneously by the patient (Desoille, 1961; Lakoff, 1980; Shone, 1988). Such amplification explicates what was implicit in the image proposed by the patient, transforming the concept into something real and condensing the most relevant inputs (Casula, 2002, 2017a).

Metaphors have the power to concentrate therapeutic messages into a few significant and evocative sentences. In order to utilize, reframe, and expand patients' metaphors, the clinician develops the ability to listen to language as an expression of a patient's idiosyncratic thinking and feeling, bringing these thoughts and feelings to the level of consciousness.

In particular, the clinician learns to distinguish a patient's personal language from the language considered part of a general idiom; that is, ready-made phrases often used in everyday language whose meanings are taken for granted (Lakoff, 1980). When listening to these words or sentences that in rhetoric are called "dead"—dead because they have lost their evocative quality to suggest unusual frames of reference or to enhance new associations of new meanings—the clinician can decide to play with them to unveil some hidden aspects, or to resurrect them with guided imagery (Casula, 1997, 2002; Perelman, 1977). Let me give an example of each case.

A patient told me that she realized that people did not always respect her boundaries. I replied, "So you don't stop them at a checkpoint and ask them for their passport and visa?" The following case shows the transformation of the patient's metaphor into guided imagery.

The Backpack

Franca (the patients' names in the case studies presented in this chapter have been changed to ensure privacy) wished to become more involved in her present experience, free of remorse and regret. When talking about her burden, she often used the metaphor of shouldering a "huge and burdensome" backpack, which caused her to walk bending towards the ground, instead of looking proudly forward. I utilized her metaphor and treated it as if it were a real, concrete, tangible, and visible backpack.

After a trance induction, I asked her to take the backpack off and place it in front of us, so that we could explore what she had stored inside over the years. While she was exploring the contents, I suggested she should accept everything inside and feel thankful for all her experiences. I reinforced that she was in a safe place, where she could welcome the suffering of the past, knowing that it was time for her to get rid of it. Franca identified several episodes of injustice, betrayals, and disappointments. In each case, I asked her to explore what she had learned that she had not known before and would not have learned otherwise.

After removing past experiences from the backpack, I then proposed that Franca imagine a symbol for everything she had learned, and to then carry those symbols with her. After identifying a variety of learning symbols, I asked if she wanted to put her backpack on again or just leave it at my office, knowing I would take good care of it. She was free to retrieve it whenever she needed, to look inside to check if there was something that still needed to be worked on. She thought about it for a while and then concluded that from now on she no longer needed to take her backpack with her. At the end of our session, Franca recognized that she felt the lightness she had been seeking for a long time.

The clinician who experiences the healing power of metaphors has acquired the habit of collecting anecdotes, stories, and clinical cases to convey the most appropriate positive message: a unique message for a particular person in specific circumstances at that particular moment of his or her life (Peseshkian, 1979; Shah, 1970; Walls, 1985, 1991). The clinician may also have learned to construct his or her own metaphors, metaphors created with the help of basic recipes that insert the ingredients needed to attain the treatment goals. The goals, of course, being ones the clinician and patient have agreed upon together (Casula 2002; Gordon, 1978; Lankton & Lankton 1980).

The clinician can also use a metaphor to transmit his/her values without any attempt to impose them on the patient (Casula, 2009, 2011). Some articles and books offer ready-made metaphors to be selected according to a clinician's interests and values; others teach clinicians how to create our own repertoire, offering a recipe with the basic ingredients (Barker, 1996; Close, 1998; Gordon, 1978; Hammond, 1990).

The focus of this chapter is *not* on how to create metaphors, but mainly on how to use what the patient brings to the session, while, at the same time, strengthening the therapeutic alliance and entering into greater resonance with the patient's inner world. This way of utilizing, reframing, and expanding a patient's own metaphor by creating guided imagery is based on the principle of transforming the patient's world into a concrete and externalized representation of something else, thus inviting the patient to explore its hidden potential to give a different meaning to his or her experience (Short & Casula, 2004; Short et al., 2005).

Guided imagery can also be a way to provide therapeutic suggestions via indirect messages. The difference between a metaphor as a story and guided imagery is that in the metaphor we talk about a protagonist who has a problem and who, in order to solve it, overcomes difficulties and learns what to do differently. On the other hand, with guided imagery, the clinician invites the patient to leave the patient's creative unconscious mind free to imagine what might happen in the future or might have happened in the past. In proposing a guided fantasy, the clinician selects the most generative aspects of the metaphor presented by the patient, relegating to the background those aspects with previously negative connotations. This reframing is reinforced by multiple suggestions that invite the patient to adopt different points of view.

Both in the case of a metaphor as a story and in that of a metaphor as a guided fantasy, the clinician can adopt and therefore stimulate various styles of thought in the patient. In this way, the clinician can reframe the meaning of the presenting problem or possible solution, as proposed by the patient. The clinician can intertwine magical thinking with empathy and scientific knowledge, laws of nature with philosophy, myth with religion, and historical figures with archetypes. The clinician can also create a story tailored to the patient's needs, using hypnotic language enriched by suggestions, permissions, and ego-strengthening messages, following creative imagination and lateral thinking.

When the patient uses a creative metaphor to express his or her mood, the clinician can utilize this to start a guided imagery experience, as in the following cases.

Going to the Moon

I remember the case of a patient who said that, when she lost her patience and got angry, she "rocketed to the moon." I took her sentence literally, and after a trance induction I asked her to prepare herself for the long trip to the moon in her spaceship. And, once she arrived there, to be ready to admire the wonderful landscape not visible from any place on Earth. On the moon she could observe the earth and its characteristics: earth and water, sky and stars, rivers and oceans, hills and mountains, deserts and green valleys.

While admiring the earth from the perspective of the moon, she could also imagine how many people inhabit the planet in each specific area. She could also reflect on the nuances and details lost at such a distance: every particularity of the earth is blurred, everything seems to dissolve in a cloud of indifference. After having explored the earth overall from the moon, she could then zoom her attention onto Europe, Italy, Lombardy, and Milan; find the street where she lives, her condominium and her apartment. Keeping the moon-earth distance, she could now observe what was happening in her home from a detached perspective and with better understanding of the global *picture*.

The Tame Devil

The following case represents another way of helping a patient to reframe a label-metaphor regarding her identity through guided imagery.

This is the story of Anna, who was verbally abusive with her partner. Her need for attention and recognition was never satiated. As soon as her partner did not react in the way she wanted, she thought he did not love her anymore and wanted to leave her. She needed endless proof that her partner loved her. When she was not able to calm down, she insulted him with bad language. Her companion told her that he did not want to accept her verbal abuse anymore. He knew that he loved her, but he was not willing to endure this kind of unjustified mistreatment. She came to me with the aim to learn how to calm herself, becoming aware of the "real" situation. She realized that she was overreacting, and that there were no sound reasons to distrust her companion's dedication.

During one hypnotic session Anna remembered that, when she was little, because of her tantrums, her grandmother gave her the epithet of "indemoniata," which means possessed by the devil. I felt that this was a good metaphor to be therapeutically utilized and reframed it with the externalization technique (Short & Casula, 2004; Short et al., 2005).

Thus, I asked her to enter the trance state of being "indemoniata" and imagine feeling, hearing, and meeting the devil who possessed her. When she entered that state she felt a strong sensation on her back, as if a giant was overwhelming and dominating her, looming over her, telling her what was going on was not right, and she had to defend herself fiercely.

Since this sensation and the voice came from her back, she could not see the devil. So I suggested that she turn around in order to confront him directly. After overcoming her fear, she turned around and saw an indistinct big black figure. I proposed for her to observe him more closely in order to look directly at his face and eyes. She told me that there was no face; it was like a big black plastic indistinct figure, like a balloon, with no identity, without any face.

I asked her what she wanted to do with that figure. She told me she felt the impulse to puncture him. I told her to imagine doing it. She did, and then imagined that the shapeless black figure collapsed on the ground. In a short while, all her fear had vanished. She started laughing and I reinforced her laughter, ratifying her experience with different sounds of acknowledgement like, "Hmm… hmm," and saying, "It's all right…" "Very good…"

When she stopped laughing, I asked her what she wanted to do with the black plastic thing on the floor, and she responded that she could jump on it. And she did. After this guided imagery, she was able to replace the aggressive devil with an inspiring daemon to reach eudaimonia, or happiness, in her relationship with her partner.

The Healing Ring

The following case represents a way of utilizing a simple object brought by the patient and reframing it with healing power.

Francesca came looking for help for a candida infection which, according to her gynecologist, had lasted longer than expected due to psychological reasons. During our first two sessions we explored the hypothetical reasons for the infection and its secondary gains. At our third session, Francesca started by telling me that she had come to the session wearing a ring she used to wear before suffering from candida. It was a ring she had not worn for a long time.

During this session we identified her resources thanks to her magic ring.

Following the utilization attitude, I suggested closing her eyes and caressing her ring, knowing that it contained all the knowledge she was looking for. I continued asking the ring to remind Francesca of how she had lived her without candida; what had she liked doing the most, who were her friends, what kind of activities did they do together, and how had she spent her free time. I suggested she should explore what she had felt most frequently, how she had imagined her life, what fantasies and projects she had had, what emotions she had felt most often, and what meaning she had given to her life.

After that induction with the magic ring that knew her previous resources, talents, and secrets, Francesca realized that she had recently been neglecting herself, had stopped listening to her own deepest desires, and had instead tried to please her lover who demanded total dedication from her.

The Statue of Responsibility

The following case shows a mixture of metaphors, such as an anecdote and guided imagery.

Giovanni came to therapy with the intention of learning how to control his rage. He expressed uncontrollable anger, especially when he was driving and someone in front of him did something wrong or dangerous. Several times he followed the car and sometimes stopped suddenly just in front of it, got out, and approached the driver; shouting menacingly and threatening to beat him. Fortunately, until now, he had always found reasonable persons who did not escalate the fight, and he was able to leave without further negative consequences. He told me that his main reason for attacking strangers who dared to cross his path was rooted in the principle of his freedom to defend himself from abuse.

Actually, for many years he had been a victim of abuse and he felt he had acquired the right of self-defense as just compensation for his history.

Giovanni knew that his behavior was risky and dangerous and he was motivated to stop it. I agreed with him and quoted Aristotle: "Those who do not know their limits, fear destiny."

I first needed to help him to recover from past traumas, such as neglect and beatings by his mother, and the rape by a transsexual who infected him with HIV while he was drunk.

When he gained the ability to put his past traumas into the past without resentment and rancor, I moved his attention to his present life and discovered that he was not satisfied with his job. I suggested he should update his CV and encouraged him to search for a more satisfying job.

After that, we worked on his future without anger. And when he expressed his intention to marry and have children, we talked about the need for social responsibility. In a search for the resources that may be available to him, I asked him about times when he was able to calm down while driving. He told me it had happened once when he saw that the person driving badly was an old man who reminded him of his father. For this person, he felt understanding and compassion instead of anger and disgust. I wanted to reinforce his inner seed of compassion and awaken his wise heart by telling him the following true story, paraphrased from one described by Jack Kornfield (Kornfield, 2009).

The Veteran

A veteran returns from war unable to govern his impulses of anger, so he goes to a monk to ask for help. The monk greets him with loving kindness and makes him understand that he can contain his aggression by concentrating his attention on his breathing and immersing himself in thoughts of acceptance and compassion. As soon as he realizes that something irritates him, he can concentrate his attention on his breath so as to calm down and understands that he is only being disturbed by a detail while ignoring the larger picture to which that detail belongs. Focusing on breathing helps him to remain calm, to observe what is happening around him, and to gather other elements that allow him to understand that the detail making him angry belongs to a larger reality.

Once, in a supermarket, the young man finds an opportunity to put into practice the indications of the monk. While standing in line, he notices an elderly woman in front of him holding a little child. The old woman has only one small item to buy but, instead of paying and leaving immediately, she gives the child to the cashier, who cuddles him a bit and then returns him to the woman. The veteran feels his anger rising and he would like to bark at the old woman to hurry up, pay quickly and leave the place to other people standing in line; he also would like to tell the cashier to do her job without wasting the customers' time. Instead, remembering the wise words of the monk and his promise to him, the veteran takes long deep breaths, practices patience, and waits quietly observing. When his turn comes, the veteran tells the cashier that the child was really cute. And she answers: "Thank you. He is my son. My husband died recently in the war and I have to work. My mother takes care of him and twice a day she comes here to let me see my little baby and cuddle him a little."

Giovanni felt moved by this true story and told me that he wanted to become a better man and learn to behave in a responsible way. I focused my interventions on how not to personalize, to understand that strangers who cut in his way while he is driving his car do not think in the least to harm him, but only about being in a hurry and their needs. I reinforced the concept by using the metaphor that each of us is a grain of sand in the midst of many grains of sand that coexist in a space too narrow for some of us.

During the first session after the Christmas holidays he told me that he had spent New Year's Eve in New York, where he asked his partner to marry him and she accepted. He was very happy. In New York they went to visit the Statue of Liberty and he was impressed by this symbol of freedom and opportunity, standing so strait with a torch in one hand, and with one foot forward in a walking position. We were talking about this when he told me that he would like to combine freedom and opportunity with responsibility.

After recognizing that we didn't know of any statue to responsibility, I asked him to close his eyes and to imagine being a sculptor who wanted to make a statue representing responsibility. I gave him time to build his statue, giving him permissive suggestions regarding his freedom to select materials, colors, overall shape, and symbols. When he gave me a non-verbal sign that he had completed his statue, I asked him to select a place where to put it.

During debriefing, after the end of the formal hypnotic session, he told me that he had created a big and colorful statue of a strong and solid man holding a small child on his left arm and a dog on a leash in the right hand. He ended his imagined work by placing his Statue of Responsibility alongside of the Statue of Liberty, so that, from now on, freedom and responsibility would no longer be separated, but combined.

The Door of Freedom

Other times, when I want to encourage patients to take responsibility for their own lives, I tell them the following story (Casula 2017b).

During a war, a general was in charge of taking care of the prisoners. Before deciding what to do with them, the general would lead the newly captured to a heavy iron door with blood-covered bodies painted on it. There he would say, "You can decide whether to remain here as a prisoner or go through that door, after which you cannot return."

Most chose to remain where they were as prisoners.

After the war was over and all the prisoners were ready to be liberated, one of them asked the general what was behind the door.

"Freedom," replied the general.

Conclusion

In this chapter, I have proposed several ways of using patients' metaphors, with the intention of helping them to gain flexibility in their way of perceiving, feeling, and attributing meaning to what happens in their lives. Metaphors, anecdotes, and guided imagery belong to the helpful family of indirect techniques that can be used to send hidden therapeutic suggestions. In particular, I showed in some clinical cases how to transform a metaphor used by a patient into a concrete base for an imaginary journey into the unconscious mind, and into its resources.

References

Barker, P. (1996). *Psychotherapeutic metaphors: A guide to theory and practice*. Bristol, PA: Brunner/Mazel

Casula, C. C. (2002). *Giardinieri, principesse, porcospini: Metafore per l'evoluzione personale e professionale*. Milan, Italy: Franco Angeli.

Casula, C. C. (1997). *I porcospini di Schopenhauer: Come condurre gruppi di formazione*. Milan, Italy: Franco Angeli.

Casula, C. C. (2017a). *La ciotola d'oro: Vivere il presente, imparare dal passato, progettare il futuro in terapia.* Milan, Italy: Mimesis.

Casula, C, C. (2011). *La forza della vulnerabilità: Utilizzare la resilienza per superare le avversità.* Milan, Italy: Franco Angeli.

Casula, C. C. (2009). *Le scarpe della principessa: Donne e l'arte di diventare se stesse (a cura di).* Milan, Italy: Franco Angeli.

Casula, C. C. (2017b). *Meditazioni guidate* [CD]. Milan, Italy: Red!

Close, H. T. (1998). *Metaphor in psychotherapy: Clinical applications of stories and allegories.* Oakland, CA: Impact Publishers

Desoille, R. (1961). *Theorie et pratique du Reve Eveille Dirige.* Geneva, Switzerland: Editions du Mont-Blanc.

Gordon, D. (1978). *Therapeutic metaphors: Helping others through the looking glass.* Tucson, AZ: Meta Publication.

Hammond, C. D. (1990). *Handbook of hypnotic suggestions and metaphors.* New York, NY: WW Norton.

Kornfield, J. (2009). *The wise heart: A guide to the universal teachings of Buddhist psychology.* New York, NY: Bantam Books.

Lakoff, G., & Johnson, M. (1980). *Metaphors we live by.* Chicago, IL: The University of Chicago Press.

Lankton, C. H., & Lankton, S. R. (1989). *Tales of enchantment: Goal-oriented metaphors for adults and children in therapy.* Bristol, PA: Brunner/Mazel.

Perelman C. 1977. *L'empire rhétorique: Rhétorique et argumentation.* Paris, France: Libraire Philosophique.

Peseschkian, N. (1979). *Oriental stories as tools in psychotherapy.* Berlin, Germany: Springer-Verlag.

Shah, I. (1970). *Tales of dervishes*. London, United Kingdom: E.P. Dutton.

Shone, R. (1988). *Creative visualization*. Rochester, VT: Desitny Books.

Short, D., Erickson, B. A., & Klein, R. E. (2005). *Hope and resiliency: Understanding the psychotherapeutic strategies of Milton H. Erickson*. Carmarthen, UK: Crown House Publishing.

Short, D., & Casula, C. C. (2004). *Speranza e resilienza: Cinque strategie terapeutiche di Milton H. Erickson*. Milan, Italy: Franco Angeli.

Wallas, L. (1985). *Stories for the third ear*. New York, NY: WW Norton.

Wallas, L. (1991). *Stories that Heal: Reparenting adult children of dysfunctional families using hypnotic stories in psychotherapy*. New York, NY: WW Norton.

CHAPTER 9

The Hypnotic Trance Space Theory (Matsuki Method): Clinicians and Patients Working Together to Build a Therapeutic Trance "Space"

Shigeru Matsuki

Shigeru Matsuki, clinical psychologist, is a professor at Hanazono University in Kyoto, Japan. He is currently the chair of the Japanese Society of Clinical Hypnosis and executive director of the Japanese Society of Hypnosis. Based on his more than 40 years of experience in the application of clinical hypnosis, he regularly applies hypnosis in his psychotherapy practice and studies its effects in both hospital and private practice settings. His field of practice is broad, including the treatment of psychiatric symptoms (e.g., anxiety disorder, dissociative disorder, personality disorder), psychosomatic disorders (IBS, chronic pain), a variety of additional medical conditions (e.g., type 1 diabetes, dystonia, juvenile Parkinson's disease), and general stress in both adults and children. He is the author of numerous articles and books, including many on the topic of stress management in children, as well as publications regarding his theory of "the space of hypnotic trance," which is a model for how hypnotherapy has its healing effects.

*   *   *

What most clinicians think of when treating patients with hypnosis is how to efficiently build a hypnotic state that will facilitate the patient's inner process for solving their presenting problem. Furthermore, one of our most important tasks in therapy is to support our patients' "correct way of struggle" (Masui, 1987), a way that often emerges when the patient is in a hypnotic state. These factors are essential when considering how hypnosis facilitates healing.

Empathy and clinician-patient resonance are prerequisites for hypnosis to evoke its healing effects. Hypnosis is not a one-way communication; it is a *mutual* communication between the patient and the clinician. How the patient experiences the whole hypnotic session—including the induction—is critically important and will strongly affect the course of the therapy.

The Basis of the Matsuki Method

Nurtured by these working hypotheses, the Matsuki Method is composed of three general principles.

1. The hypnotic trance is viewed as an imaginary "space," mutually created by the cooperative work of the clinician and the patient. The hypnotic induction is all about building this safe "place" between the two participants, and the clinician must recognize that in building a "mutual place," he or she must listen to the other's opinions and desires to make the "place" safe for both. In practicing the *Matsuki Method*, the clinician's empathic response and the interaction between the clinician and the patient are essential; factors not always considered important in traditional hypnosis. Thus, an effective hypnotic induction does

not involve a stereotypical induction script that is provided in a directive manner. *The induction itself is already part of the intervention.* Therefore, collaborative work is required.

2. If this "space" is the fruit that emerges from the interaction between the clinician and patient, both play a critical role in building it. In contrast to traditional hypnosis where the patient remains passive (the phrase "be hypnotized" explains it all), the patient actively participates in building this mutual space; more specifically, the *way* the patient experiences the induction changes at a certain point during the hypnotic induction. At first, the patient may feel as if he or she is "being hypnotized," but this shifts to "actively commits to building the hypnotic trance." This is where the patient changes his or her attitude toward the hypnotic session. It is important to observe the signs that make each session effective. It is always the interaction between the clinician and the patient that evokes this change in the patient's commitment to hypnosis.

3. Whatever response the patient shows during the hypnotic induction is a message provided by the patient; it can be utilized as a resource for producing therapeutic change, or it might provide a clue for a deeper understanding of the patient's problem. It could even be both. Either way, how the clinician deals with these messages from the patient defines the course of therapy. The messages provide the clinician with important hints for devising the most effective suggestions. In other words, every suggestion is something that spontaneously arises in the clinician as

a result of the interaction between the patient and clinician, and this will always reflect the inner state of the patient. Communicating such suggestions will help patients connect with their internal selves to further understand their presenting problem, hopefully also discovering their resources for solving it. Therefore, in practicing the Matsuki Method, the clinician must recognize suggestion as a communication tool, a tool that the patient can use to promote new perceptions and new resources.

The Philosophy Behind the Theory

Although the Matsuki Method shares some common features with Milton Erickson's approach to hypnosis, it was born on different soil, as was the philosophy that underlies the approach. The idea of building a "place" arose from ideas mainly understood in eastern philosophy, ideas such as "*Ji-ta hi-bunri*" (non-separation of the self and the other; Nishida, 1991), "*Dou-teki Chou-wa*" (the balance is achieved by the dynamic interaction of the two; Nakamura, 2000), and "*Kankeisei-jyushi*" (emphasizing relationship rather than independence; Itasaka, 1971; Matsuki, 1998). It is also influenced by mind-body monism theories (Ichikawa, 1984; Merleau-Ponty, 1933). From this view, the Matsuki Method may be seen as a type of holistic medicine; it assumes that the power to heal lies within every patient and seeks to use hypnosis to help patients access their inner resources.

The Process of Building the "Space"

Figures 9.1 through 9.4 illustrate the four steps involved when building the trance "space" using the Matsuki Method.

The first step can be described as a state where the "trance space is not (yet) shared between the clinician and the patient" (see Figure 9.1). In this state, the patient feels as if he or she is "being hypnotized." The relationship between the clinician and the patient could be described as the clinician being dominant and manipulative; the patient just "sits passively" during the process, not actively participating in the experience. As long as the patient remains passive in this way, the clinician cannot facilitate the healing process.

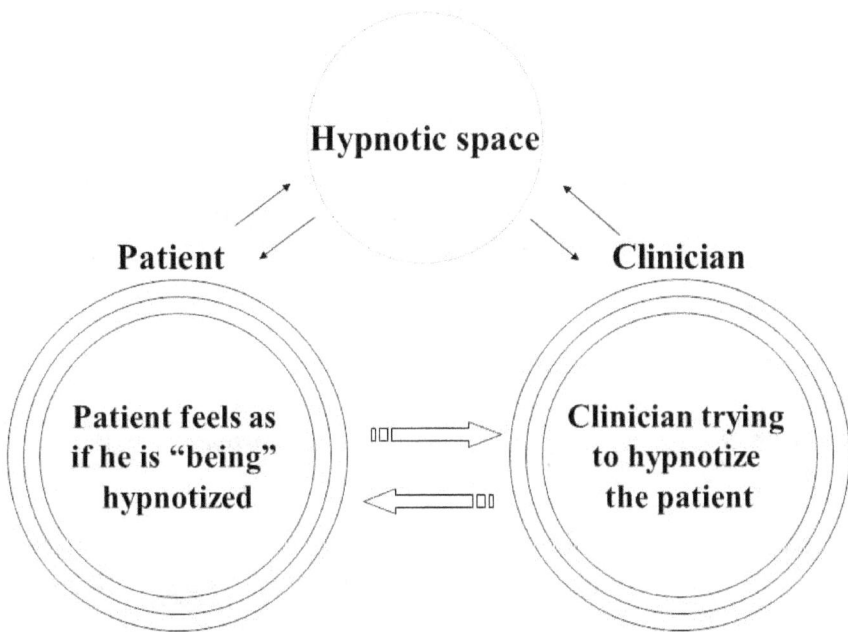

Hypnotic space

Patient   **Clinician**

Patient feels as if he is "being" hypnotized   **Clinician trying to hypnotize the patient**

Figure 9.1. Trance "space" is not being shared between the clinician and the patient (first step).

In order to facilitate movement from this step towards healing, the clinician's task at this stage is to interact with the patient in a way that their response to hypnosis is not suppressed; specifically, the clinician should accept and utilize any response that the patient shows. If this is not achieved, the patient may have an adverse reaction. In fact, it is the failure to move from this first step that accounts for most, if not all, of the adverse reactions to hypnosis. Thus, it is crucial to move beyond this step in order to prevent harm.

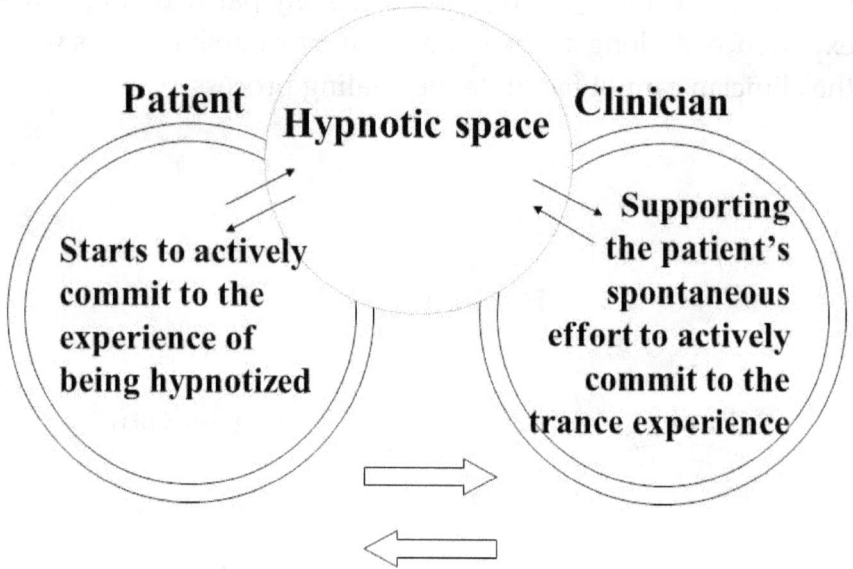

Figure 9.2. Patient and clinician are about the share the trance experience (second step).

Steps two, three, and four show how the relationship between the patient and the clinician changes during the hypnotic intervention from step one, resulting in a therapeutic space being built. Figure 9.2 can be described as a state where "the patient and clinician are about to share the trance experience." This proceeds to a relationship where "the patient and clinician are both sharing a stable trance experience" (see Figure 9.3), and finally to a state where "an empathic trance 'space' is mutually built by the patient and the clinician" (see Figure 9.4).

Patient **Clinician**

Effortlessly accepting the hypnotic experience

Hypnotic space

Accepting the patient's active commitment to the trance experience

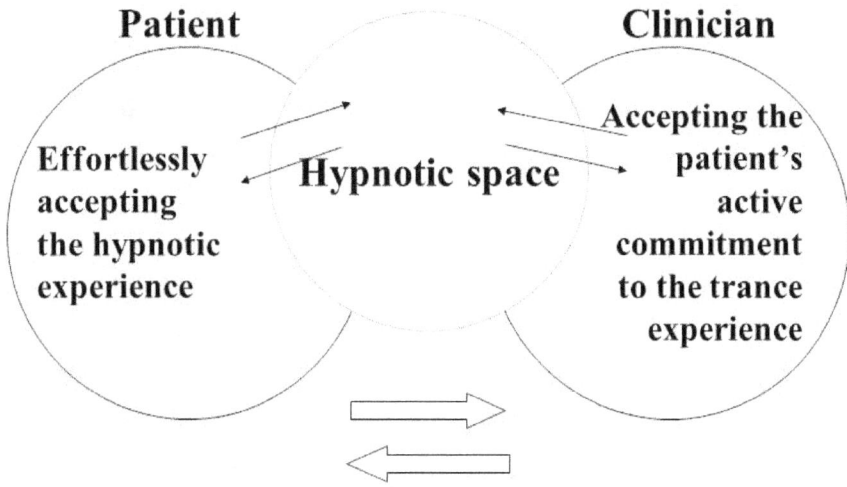

Figure 9.3. Patient are clinician share a stable trance experience (third step).

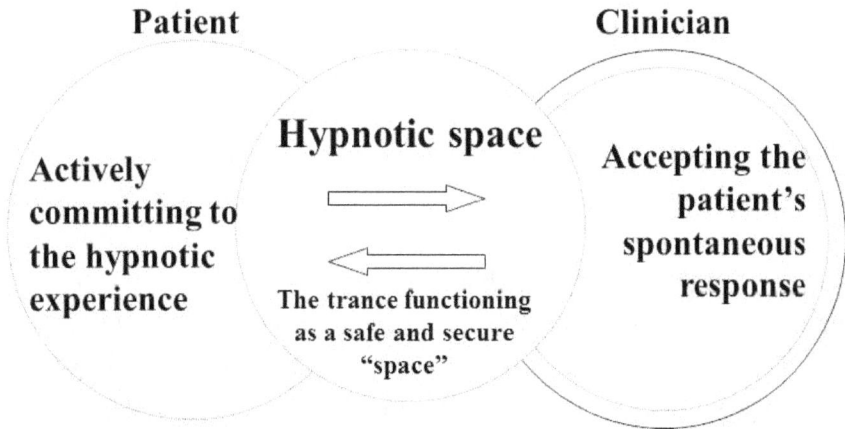

Patient **Clinician**

Hypnotic space

Actively committing to the hypnotic experience

The trance functioning as a safe and secure "space"

Accepting the patient's spontaneous response

Figure 9.4. An emphatic trance "space" is mutually built by the patient and clinician (fourth step).

Naruse (1992) argues that the healing mechanism of hypnosis lies largely in changes in *how* a patient experiences clinical events. The Matsuki Method targets this new experience, maximizing the healing power of hypnosis by focusing on the clinician-patient empathic interaction. As the patient and clinician work through the four steps, the patient will start to respond differently, showing that the patient is experiencing the hypnotic process differently. This enlists the resources within the patient to address the presenting problem(s).

Thus, our primary goal is to support the patient in a way that allows him or her to actively participate in building this safe and secure space; where the patient is permitted to freely experience and explore their inner resources, nurturing the patient's ability to discover and then utilize these resources. In other words, aimlessly exposing patients to their weaknesses is never going to be effective. The clinician must always respect the patient's spontaneous efforts to solve their problem (even when these efforts do not look so nice!); efforts that naturally emerge during the entire hypnotic procedure.

Let's take a deeper look at Figure 9.4. It is typical that in step four, while the clinician is observing the patient, the clinician is also in a light trance, being open to sharing a part of the patient's hypnotic experience (as indicated by the dotted line on the clinician's side). Together, the patient and the clinician "melt into" the space, as if both lose their ego borders, making it difficult for either party to identify if their experience belongs to them alone, or if it is shared with the other. In contrast to step three, where the clinician interacts with the patient to support the patient's spontaneous efforts, the clinician will feel that he or she is supporting the (trait of) spontaneity inside the patient.

Some may object that "empathy" is not the correct term to describe this approach. In fact, the approach might be viewed from the psychoanalytical concept of "affect attunement" (Stern, 1985) or "participant observation" (Sullivan, 1968); or, as described by Winnicott (2005) as, "Here in this area of overlap between the playing of the child and the playing of the other person there is a chance to introduce enrichments" (p. 50).

This approach also shares many features with Milton Erickson's use of hypnosis, such as frequent use of permissive language (O'Hanlon, 1992), or the way Erickson emphasizes the importance of respecting each unique patient (Zeig, 1985). Thus, it is certainly possible that there might be a concept or a theory that explains this general approach as being something more than empathy. In any case, the key issue in the clinical application of the Matsuki Method is the focus on building this healing space with the help of hypnosis; a space where patients are allowed to safely discover their internal resources for solving their own problems.

Example Script of the Matsuki Method

The key principal in practicing the Matsuki Method is communicating with the patient during the whole hypnotic session (from the beginning of the induction to finally alerting), with a focus on examining how the patient is experiencing the hypnotic trance. This allows the patient to safely enter trance at their initiative. This means a clear avoidance of a standardized script. Thus, in this section I provide an example script with detailed commentary describing my intentions during the hypnotic session. However, the script is not meant to be read to a patient verbatim.

Figure 9.5 illustrates the process of how traditional hypnosis is performed. However, since I view the patient's response at each phase as an indirect communication to the clinician, the way the clinician responds to each message will have a significant impact on the patient's whole hypnotic experience. Thus, *the induction phase is already a part of the clinical intervention, as are the clinical suggestion phase and even the alerting phase.* This is represented in Figure 9.5 by the phrase, *"CLINICAL INTERVENTION,"* which is a part of each stage.

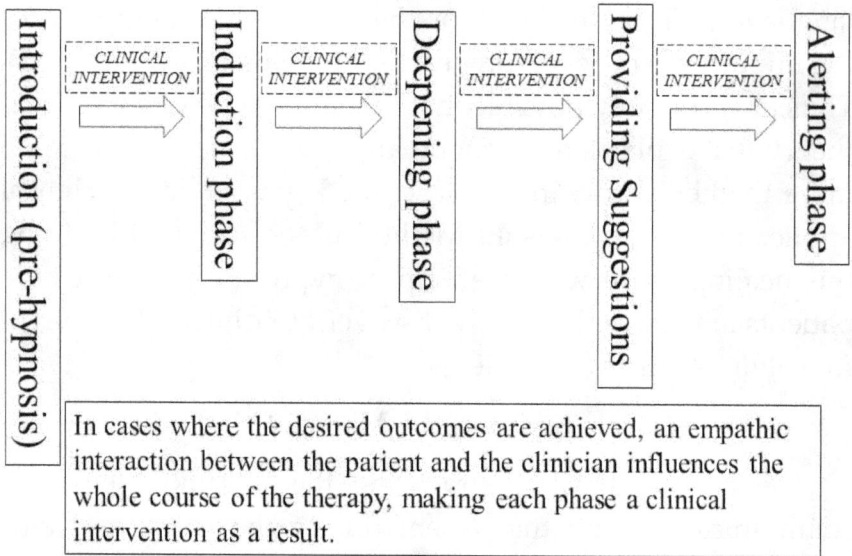

In cases where the desired outcomes are achieved, an empathic interaction between the patient and the clinician influences the whole course of the therapy, making each phase a clinical intervention as a result.

Figure 9.5. How hypnosis is done with an emphasis on the patient-clinician relationship.

For example, let's take a look at a simple arm drop induction. The clinician might say, "As you focus on your right/left arm, it might become heavy and begin to drop." Many patients will respond to the induction as suggested. But there are also many times when the patient shows different reactions. One might develop arm catalepsy; another might respond with arm levitation. In other cases, if the clinician suggests hypnotic relaxation as a component of the induction, some patients might start to panic.

These are just few simple examples of how patients vary in their responses to inductions. A large variety of responses will also be observed when clinical suggestions are offered. One patient might show strong affective responses (crying, anger expression), while another might have motor responses (catalepsy, adynamia, involuntary movements). The patient might show autonomic nervous system changes (change in respiration or body temperature), sensory responses (numbness, pain), visual or sensory images, and so on. These are all indirect messages that the patient is sending to the clinician.

In some cases, the message might be telling us something about the core of the presenting problem, or the patient's current way of coping with it. The message might be communicating something about the patient's core values or general approach. Therefore, the clinician should always closely observe each unique response, and ask him or herself, "Why is this patient responding in this way? What is he or she communicating to me?" Clinicians who do this are in a better position to respond empathically and guide the patient, so that the patient's responses can be more effectively utilized to solve the problem.

Case Presentation

The case I present here is a 30-year-old man who had been diagnosed with social anxiety disorder with a serious stutter. During our initial interview he did not speak about the core issues that were related to his presenting symptoms. But I assumed that there were import issues that lay behind the symptoms as I began the induction.

For the induction, we discussed and agreed to use the arm drop method. Contrary to my expectation, his arm did not descend at first; it showed catalepsy instead. His hand then started to shake, and his arm dropped just a little bit as he took a deep breath. Then the arm stopped dropping once again.

This cycle was repeated several times. As I observed his response, I noticed that the catalepsy was not only present in his arm, but also in his throat; as he breathed, the two (catalepsy of the arm and the throat) seemed to respond synchronically.

It can easily be assumed from this reaction that the patient felt nervous at all times and was not used to relaxing his muscles. But this phenomenon can also be understood as psychological resistance (to the suggestion that his arm drop) which could mean that he experiences a conflict in psychologically "lowering his arms."

As is the case in English, the body part "arm" is used in many idioms in Japanese. In Japanese, the arm tends to be used as a metaphor representing one's skills, as well as the quality of one's interpersonal relationships. Thinking in terms of skills, a resistance to dropping the arm could mean that the patient is afraid he might be losing important skills (*"ude-ga sagaru"* is Japanese for "dropping one's arms" and is used as an idiom for losing one's skill). In addition, and thinking in terms of interpersonal relationships, it could mean that he is having a hard time *"laying his arm"* on (i.e., maintaining) his relationships with others. A similar set of metaphors is associated with the reaction of his throat. Because of the catalepsy, he was literally a person who could not *"catch his breath,"* and/or who leaves many things *"below his breath"* (there are similar idioms in Japanese as well as in English that use the word "breath" to express interpersonal relationships).

Of course, when we receive such "resistant" responses, we could interrupt the session and discuss the patient's responses with him or her. Alternatively, we can just continue with a standardized procedure and finish the session without taking into account the patient's responses. But since the patient is communicating important information, why not join the conversation in the way that the patient prefers? The following script was how I actually communicated in this session.

[As the clinician notices the catalepsy in the patient's arm and throat...]

Clinician: Do you notice that your arm is not descending smoothly, as if it is stuck somewhere, then it drops a little, and gets stuck again...?

[For the initial step, I fixed his focus on the part of the body where the catalepsy is present.]

Patient: *[As he nods his head...]* **Yes...**

Clinician: Good. Now deeply observe this experience of your arm being stuck... and dropping... and being stuck... again and again...

Patient: *[As he nods his heads...]* **Okay, I will try...**

Clinician: How does it feel?

Patient: Um... *[after a pause]...* **I feel rather restless, uneasy...**

Clinician: That your arm is repetitively getting stuck and then dropping?

Patient: Yes... *[the arm starts to shake... the client takes a deep breath...]* **It's... my breath is...**

Clinician: You seem breathless to me.

Patient: Yes. This feeling is...

Clinician: Did you notice anything?

Patient: *[Pause...]* **It's... like... I feel as if something is stuck in my throat. ... It's similar to the sensation in my arm...**

Clinician: Hmm... The two sensations seem similar. ... Your throat getting stuck, and then relaxing... and getting stuck again...

Patient: Yes, something like that... *[pause]* I think my arm is getting much better...

[The arm starts to descend smoothly, and as this occurs the patient starts to breathe much easier.]

Clinician: How is your arm right now?

Patient: I'm feeling much better, moving.

Clinician: I guess you are starting to get the hang of how to drop your arm smoothly, aren't you?

Patient: Yes. ... It doesn't get stuck. This is... an interesting sensation...

Clinician: Do you feel much better if your arm drops smoothly?

Patient: Yes.

Clinician: Good. Now take as much time as you like and observe this comfortable feeling of getting the hang of how to smoothly drop your arm.

Patient: Okay. ... Hmm. ... It's really comfortable...

[The patient closes his eyes as the arm lands smoothly onto his knee. He appears to be experiencing a deep trance.]

Clinician: Great. Now close your eyes and get yourself relaxed. What you have experienced is somewhat unusual but also very relaxing. ... Notice the fact that your body has spontaneously brought you into this deep, relaxing state... and now you can take a deep, deep breath. ... Deeply... Relaxed... Comfortable sensations arising...

[The clinician sits quietly for a while as the patient enjoys his trance.]

Clinician: Today, you have discovered a very important thing. ... You might feel as if you had done nothing at all. ... But what you have discovered is remembered in your body, and even if you forget it, it will somehow spontaneously return to help you anytime you need it... [pause...] Now, let me know when you feel that you have enjoyed enough of this trance...

[Alerting procedure continues.]

When practicing the Matsuki Method, the clinician must think about the various possible ideas that the patient may be communicating with each response. At the same time, it is important to NOT come to a single conclusion. Instead, allow all possibilities to remain possible. It is wise to address the patient's hypnotic responses in a hypnotic state, because these rather ambiguous communications often expresses ideas that the patient (and even the clinician!) may not yet be aware of (Bandler, 1975). Our task is to help the patient more effectively utilize the response that they have evoked in relation to the clinician; this helps to lead both the patient and the clinician in building a safe place.

The essential task of understanding what the symptom is trying to communicate (which is *how* they experience the symptom) is a process that only the patient can perform; but understanding is achieved with the help of the clinician, who works collaboratively to build a safe place for the patient to reprocess their symptom.

After the hypnotic session described above, the patient told me that although he at first thought his stutter was the result of stressful relationships at work, he came to understand that in fact it was rooted deeply in his relationships with his family. This insight about his symptom was promoted by the reprocessing of the experience which occurred during the hypnosis session. He would not likely have been able to gain these insights if the trance space had not been a safe place for him to freely attend to his inner process.

Conclusion

I shall emphasize once again that *every single response in the trance state is a message from the patient that can be utilized.* Our task is to build a safe space in which the patient is given the freedom to communicate with the clinician. Therefore, it is essential that we respect and respond to their non-verbal messages in an empathic manner. This will nurture the patient's own healing powers.

References

Bander, R., & Grinder, J. (1975). *Patterns of the hypnotic techniques of Milton H. Erickson, M.D.* (Vol. 1). Santa Cruz, CA: Meta Publications.

Ichikawa, H. (1984). *Mi no Kouzou Shintai-ron wo koete. Bunkyo,* Tokyo: Kodansha Gakujyutsu Bunko.

Masui, T. (1987). Shoujyou ni taisuru Kanja no tekisetu na doryoku. *Journal of Japanese Clinical Psychology, 4,* 18-34.

Matsuki, S. (1998). Clinical linguistics of Japan, and Japanese model of handling "worry." *Journal of Japanese Clinical Psychology, 16,* 266-277.

Matsuki, S. (2003). A study of the role of empathy played in hypnotherapy. *Japanese Journal of Hypnosis, 47,* 1-8.

Matsuki, S. (2017). *Saimin toransu Ku-kan to Shinri ryouhou – serapisuto no shokunin waza wo manabu.* Mitaka, Tokyo: Tomi shobo.

Matsuki, S. (2018). *Muishiki ni todoku komyunike-shon tu-ru wo tukau-saimin to ime-ji no shinri rinshou.* Mitaka, Tokyo: Tomi shobo.

Merleau-Ponty,M. (1933). La nature de la perception. In Kaganoi, S (Ed.), *Chikaku no Honsho—shoki ronbun shuu*. Chiyoda, Tokyo: Hosei Daigaku shuppankyoku.

Nakamura, Y. (2000). *Kyou-tsu kankaku ron*. Chiyoda, Tokyo: Iwanami Gendai Bunko.

Nishida, K. (1991). *Zen no kenkyu*. Chiyoda, Tokyo: Ianami Shoten.

Naruse, G. (1992). *Saimin Ryouhou wo kangaeru*. Bunkyo, Tokyo: Seishin Shobo.

O'Hanlon, W. H. (1992). *Solution oriented hypnosis: An Ericksonian approach*. New York, NY: WW Norton.

Stern, D. N. (1985). *The interpersonal world of the infant: A view from psychoanalysis and developmental psychology*. New York, NY: Basic Books.

Sullivan, H. S. (1968). *The interpersonal theory of psychiatry*. New York, NY: WW Norton.

Winnicott, D. W. (2005). *Playing and reality*. Abingdon, Oxon: Routledge.

Zeig, K. (1985). *Experiencing Erickson*. Levittown, PA: Brunner/Mazel Publishers.

Sugisaka, H. (1971). *Nihon jin no ronri kouzou*. Bunkyo, Tokyo: Kodansha.

Shimizu, H. (1990). *Seimei wo torae naosu—ikiteiru jyoutai towa nani ka*. Chiyoda, Tokyo: Chu-ko Shin sho.

CHAPTER 10

Using Hypnotic Reflective Listening to Identify Effective Suggestions for Behavior Change

Mark P. Jensen

Mark P. Jensen is a professor and vice chair for research in the Department of Rehabilitation Medicine, University of Washington, Seattle, Washington, USA. For the past 40 years, his clinical work and research program have focused on developing interventions—including self-hypnosis treatment programs—that empower patients to get more control over their symptoms and health-related behaviors. He has published over 500 articles and chapters and has facilitated hundreds of workshops throughout the world for clinicians to disseminate the knowledge gained from this work. Among other awards recognizing his contributions, he has received the Jay Haley Early Career Award for Innovative Contributions to Hypnosis from The International Society of Hypnosis, the Clark L. Hull Award for Scientific Excellence in Writing on Experimental Hypnosis from the American Journal of Clinical Hypnosis, the Wilbert E. Fordyce Clinical Investigator Award from the American Pain Society, and both the Distinguished Contributions to Scientific Hypnosis and the Distinguished Contributions to Professional Hypnosis awards from the American Psychological Association, Division 30. His 2011 book, Hypnosis for Chronic Pain

Management: Therapist Guide, *published by Oxford University Press as part of their "Treatments that Work" series, won the Arthur Shapiro Award: Best Book on Hypnosis from the Society for Clinical and Experimental Hypnosis. In this chapter, Professor Jensen describes a technique—Hypnotic Reflective Listening—which can be used to identify powerful hypnotic suggestions for helping patients make behavioral changes.*

*   *   *

Hypnosis can be used effectively to help patients achieve many goals. Among the most common of these goals are behavior changes related to one's health, such as eating appropriate portions of the appropriate foods, or becoming a non-smoker (Bo et al., 2018; Green & Lynn, 2000, 2017; Mott & Roberts, 1979). Perhaps one of the reasons that hypnosis is so effective for facilitating behavior change is that the great majority of our behaviors are automatic (or unconscious, cf. Bargh, 2014; Ginot, 2017), and hypnosis is known to effectively target and change automatic/unconscious processes (Anbar, 2008; Entwistle et al., 2014; Landry et al., 2014).

Automatic Thoughts as Drivers of Automatic Emotional and Behavioral Reactions

One of the underlying principles of cognitive therapy—a mainstream therapeutic approach with proven efficacy—is that thoughts and beliefs underlie automatic reactions, including emotional and behavioral reactions to events (Hofmann et al., 2013; Lorenzo-Luaces et al., 2015). Everyone responds in their own unique way to different situations and environmental cues. Based on the principles that underlie cognitive therapy, one of the factors underlying these different responses are the thoughts elicited by a situation. So the person caught in traffic who thinks, "Oh, dang, now I'm going to be late to the meeting. I'll be embarrassed and will never get promoted; one more thing that ensures I will never be successful!", will have a different emotional and behavioral reaction to the event than the person who thinks, "Fantastic! I now have more time to practice my in-car audio lessons!"

Another key principle underlying cognitive therapy is that many, if not most, cognitive reactions to cues in the environment are *automatic*; they usually occur below our awareness. Often, what we end up being most aware of is our emotional (feeling good, neutral, or bad) and behavioral reactions (finding ourselves smoking, overeating, or avoiding exercise) to events. We are not necessarily aware of the automatic thoughts that underlie these automatic responses.

Cognitive therapy uses a rational approach to alter automatic thoughts. With cognitive therapy, patients are first taught to notice their automatic thoughts (often, through the use of diaries or worksheets) and then recognize the impact of these thoughts on emotional and behavioral reactions (Beck, 2011; Gilson et al., 2009). Patients are then taught how to evaluate their thoughts in order to determine which ones are reasonable, rational, and reassuring, and which ones are less helpful and contribute to feeling bad, or lead to behaviors inconsistent with their values or health goals.

Patients are also taught strategies for coming up with (generally, reassuring) alternative thoughts to the (generally, alarming) less than helpful ones. Over time, and with practice, this process results in an overall replacement of the less than helpful automatic thoughts with more helpful ones, resulting in improvements in the patient's day-to-day automatic responses that are influenced by these thoughts.

Although, as indicated previously, this therapeutic approach has proven efficacy (Beck & Dozois, 2011; Hanrahan et al., 2013; Mello et al., 2013), when you add hypnosis to this approach, it becomes even more effective (Kirsch et al., 1995). My working hypothesis is that the reason hypnotic cognitive therapy is more effective than traditional cognitive therapy is that hypnosis is especially effective for making rapid changes in *automatic* (i.e., unconscious, non-effortful, "fast thinking" [Kahneman, 2011]) responses. Cognitive therapy, on the other hand, makes these changes using more effortful, conscious (e.g., "slow thinking" [Kahneman, 2011]) approaches.

Given these considerations, the central ideas that underlie the hypnotic technique introduced and modeled in this chapter are the following: (1) the thoughts people have—most of which are automatic and occur below conscious awareness—can be viewed as self-suggestions; (2) the therapeutic strategies of asking open questions and reflective listening are particularly effective for (a) gaining access to those automatic thoughts (i.e., self-suggestions), and for (b) identifying effective suggestions, respectively; and (3) once the most effective suggestions are identified, they can be repeated both outside of and during formal hypnosis sessions to help patients achieve behavior change goals.

Automatic Thoughts as Self-Suggestions

Hypnotic suggestions are suggestions for a patient to experience changes in their thoughts, feelings, or behaviors. In order for the suggested changes to become durable, the suggestions must be accepted by the patient. Presumably, people who are more hypnotizable tend to accept and absorb ideas and suggestions more easily than people who are less hypnotizable. Moreover, one reason that clinicians often begin hypnosis sessions with a hypnotic induction is that such inductions are thought to increase the patient's willingness and ability to absorb the clinical suggestions that are usually offered after the induction.

A premise underlying the technique presented in this chapter is that, once accepted and absorbed, a hypnotic suggestion that is offered by the clinician and accepted by the patient becomes a thought (self-suggestion) that the patient begins to tell himself or herself; *it is the change in the patient's own self-suggestions, facilitated by the hypnotic suggestion, that is an important mechanism of hypnosis's effects.* That is, an important—if not the single most important—final common pathway for the therapeutic changes that result from psychosocial treatments (whether they be produced via hypnosis, traditional cognitive therapy, or other therapeutic approaches) is via changes in a patient's self-suggestions; the effects of hypnosis on a patient's automatic thoughts may explain, at least in part, the beneficial effects of hypnosis.

The implication of this idea—automatic thoughts as self-suggestions—is that clinicians would do well to listen very carefully to what patients are telling themselves about the presenting problem. Much of what the patient verbalizes can be viewed as self-suggestions, *already present* inside of the patient. They may be self-suggestions that support positive behavior change: "I know I can do this," or "It is time for me to become a non-smoker," or "I really, really want to have a sense of control over what I eat." Or they may be self-suggestions that interfere with behavior change: "I really should exercise more" ("should" or "must" language almost always interferes with behavior change, as discussed later in this chapter); or "If I don't stop eating so much, I will die from diabetes" (threatening language often inhibits positive change); or "I am helpless when offered cake"; or "I am going to try to stop smoking" (problems with the word "try" are well known in the hypnosis community).

Given the extent to which the thoughts and ideas that already reside in a patient drive that individual's automatic day-to-day responses (e.g., thoughts of hope versus thoughts of despair, thoughts enhancing motivation to exercise on a regular basis versus a desire to remain inactive, thoughts that facilitate an automatic response to choose and enjoy healthy foods in the correct portions versus overeating foods that contribute to illness and disease, etc.), it would seem most efficient to identify, nurture, and *strengthen adaptive self-suggestions that are already present within the patient* than to work to suggest completely new ideas. Doing this would also be entirely consistent with an Ericksonian utilization approach (Zeig, 1994).

Similarly, if a patient has an automatic self-suggestion that interferes with his or her ability to easily and automatically achieve his or her goals ("Exercise makes my pain worse!"), then knowledge regarding the presence of such a self-suggestion would allow clinicians to be better able to attach or associate a new thought to this same idea to (at worst) nullify its negative impact or (at best) create a new automatic thought that contributes to the patient's identified treatment goal(s). For example, adding the idea that "The way that I have exercised in the past..." to "... has made my pain worse" could lessen the negative impact of an "exercise makes my pain worse" self-suggestion.

Also, if a patient currently has an automatic thought that contains a useful idea coupled with an idea that nullifies or makes ineffective the useful one, the clinician can use this knowledge to design a suggestion that nurtures and strengthens the most useful component of the self-suggestion. While the less useful component might not disappear altogether (it is currently thought to be very difficult if not impossible to "erase" unhelpful self-suggestions), by strengthening the useful component, the self-suggestion has a greater opportunity to be beneficial instead of harmful.

So a patient who states the belief that "Exercise is beneficial, but it is hard," can be invited to discuss the many benefits of exercise *from their perspective* and identify factors that may make exercising regularly now challenging (i.e., morphing "hard" to "challenging" and then to "easier and easier, with practice"), thus developing and nurturing the self-suggestion that "Exercise is beneficial; and can become easier and easier, with practice." Once this idea is accepted by the patient, they repeat it as an automatic thought; as result, they will likely find themselves exercising more.

Critically, in order to utilize and slightly change, if needed, the automatic thoughts that already reside within the patient, the clinician needs to invite the patient to discuss and express his or her thoughts about his or her treatment goal(s). This is where the therapeutic skills of open questions and reflective listening come in.

Open Questions and Reflective Listening

Open Questions

In order to understand the patient's self-suggestions/automatic thoughts around a topic, the clinician needs to encourage the patient to talk about the topic. The classic therapeutic skills of (1) asking open questions and (2) reflective listening, are particularly effective in achieving this goal.

Open questions are questions that cannot be answered with a single-word response. Closed questions, on the other hand, tend to elicit very few words, or sometimes even just one-word responses. Examples of closed questions around the topic of exercise include: (1) "How often do you usually exercise?" (2) "Would you like to exercise more often?" (3)

"Do you think exercise would help you to sleep better?" and (4) "How many times a week would you like to exercise?" Closed questions are not very useful for eliciting information regarding the content of the patient's self-suggestions.

Open questions, on the other hand, elicit sentences and paragraphs. The responses to open questions can provide the clinician with a wealth of information regarding the patient's inner helpful self-suggestions, as well as their less useful self-suggestions. This provides the clinician with information about the thoughts within the patient that can be utilized, nurtured, and strengthened. It also provides information about thoughts that may need modification so as to either limit their negative effects, or transform them in more useful self-suggestions.

Examples of open questions regarding exercise are: (1) "Tell me your thoughts about the role that exercise does have, and could have, in your life," (2) "I wonder, what do you see as the benefits of exercise on your own health?" (3) "What are your very favorite forms of exercise, and why do you like them?" and (4) "What are your ideas for making exercise a more regular part of your day-to-day life?"

Interested readers might ask these four closed and the four open questions one after another of a friend, and notice the differences in the responses that each type of question elicits. Also, for any reader that performs this exercise, pay very close attention to the specific language used by the friend or colleague; you will likely immediately see how the particular words used by the friend or colleague are closely linked to their actual exercise behavior.

Reflective Listening

Reflective listening involves noticing what the patient has communicated and reflecting back some or all of the ideas or feelings expressed. Because human communication is complex, a great deal of both verbal and nonverbal information is communicated during any interaction. Thus, the clinician has a great deal of latitude regarding what specific aspects of the patient's communication to reflect (Gordon, 1970; Miller & Rollnick, 2013; Roders, 1951).

Importantly, *the reflection provided by the clinician can be viewed as a suggestion.* And the patient's verbal and nonverbal response to that reflection/suggestion tells the clinician how well that reflection/suggestion will be accepted by the patient. Thus, in the context of Hypnotic Reflective Listening, described in the next section, the clinician can view each reflective statement as a "trial run" of a potential hypnotic suggestion, offered outside of the context of a formal hypnotic session. Depending on the patient's response (outright disagreement and resistance, a scowl with hesitant agreement, or visible relief and enthusiastic endorsement of the idea), the clinician gets immediate feedback regarding which one (or more) of a variety of different reflective statements might be useful as suggestions to be offered during a more formal hypnosis session.

So, for example, a patient who says, "I would like to exercise more, but I just don't have time," might be offered the reflection "You are looking for ways to find time to exercise." One patient might respond to this reflection with a scowl and say, "Not really. Why bother—I am way too busy to exercise." Another might respond with clear excitement and say, "Yes. I really want to find a way to fit exercise in my life." For the former patient, it would not likely be useful to offer hypnotic suggestions during a formal hypnosis session focusing on finding time to exercise—such suggestions would likely result in, at best, an internal conflict between the patient's current self-suggestions and the suggestion offered by the clinician. At worst, such suggestions might undermine rapport and elicit outright resistance. However, hypnotic suggestions regarding finding the time to exercise might be very effective for the second patient. In both cases, the reflection elicited a response from the patient that provides important information useful for informing the decisions regarding suggestions.

Hypnotic Reflective Listening

Hypnotic Reflective Listening involves two phases. The first phase involves asking open questions and providing reflective listening. Open questions elicit information regarding the patient's automatic thoughts about the topic at hand. Reflective listening builds rapport, encourages further discussion, and can be used to evaluate the potential acceptability and appropriateness of hypnotic suggestions that could be offered during the formal hypnotic phase. During Phase 1, the clinician may also choose to negotiate with the patient the specific hypnotic suggestions that might be offered during Phase 2—the formal hypnosis session. During Phase 1, the patient should be doing most of the talking.

The second phase of Hypnotic Reflective Listening is a more formal hypnotic session, involving an induction (if appropriate) followed by the provision of the hypnotic suggestions that were identified as most effective during Phase 1. Suggestions based on reflections that appeared to be most acceptable to the patient during Phase 1, which are then offered during Phase 2, are particularly effective because they use the patient's own words, which reduces resistance. Why would the patient resist suggestions that reflect what he or she already believes? Importantly, these reflections/suggestions utilize, nurture and strengthen ideas that already exist inside the patient. An example of a script using the two-phase Hypnotic Reflective Listening technique is presented next.

Hypnotic Reflective Listening Transcript with Commentary

The transcript that follows came from a workshop demonstration. In this case, the workshop participant ("patient" in the transcript) wanted to increase the number of times she exercised every week.

Phase 1: Open questions and reflective listening

Mark Jensen (MJ): So, tell me about what you would like to do more easily?

Patient: What I would like to do more easily is exercise every day.

MJ: Okay.

Patient: I have been increasing my exercise—significantly—I would say in the last six months or so. So that means... 45 minutes usually. I usually use a recumbent bike, or I go for a walk. I *aim* for 45 minutes every day, but I don't get there. And sometimes it's as little as two or three times a week.

MJ: 45 minutes... every day.

> *[Reflecting the patient's goal using the patient's own words. By reflecting what the patient has communicated, the clinician builds rapport, increasing readiness to respond to the ideas and suggestions that will be offered during the discussion, as well as during the more formal hypnosis session. However, even as I reflected this (and perhaps in part **because** I said it myself), I was aware of my own resistance to the idea of needing to exercise for 45 minutes **every day**.*

That sounded like a lot to me, and I immediately experienced my own sense of ambivalence about this goal, perhaps an ambivalence that is something like the patient experiences. So at this point I already had a session goal of eliciting the patient's thoughts about whether this is an ideal goal, considering feasibility and her own reasons for exercising more. Perhaps having a goal of exercising regularly, but less often than every day, might be more feasible and therefore ultimately more successful for this patient.]

Patient: Probably two times a week if I'm really busy, if I've got work and commitments. Somehow I use that as an excuse.

[The word "excuse," so soon in the discussion, made me think that this patient may be more self-critical than may be helpful for her. If there are self-suggestions that are "nagging" and saying that one "should" or "must" do this or that, this usually elicits guilt feelings. And guilt inhibits behavior change (Miller & Rollnick, 2013). So at this point I also had a goal to work with the part (ego state) of the patient that may be self-critical, to help her learn more helpful ways to motivate healthy behavior; to offer the patient self-suggestions that elicit hope, optimism, and feelings of self-efficacy, rather than guilt.]

Patient continues: Well, "You have work to do."

[The part of the patient that is not ready to exercise every day is given voice. It is important to listen carefully to this voice and take it into account in order to negotiate hypnotic suggestions with the patient that are going to be most readily accepted by all of the patient's ego states. I therefore reflected this important idea to indicate support for this important value.]

MJ: Yeah. You have important commitments.

*[Ultimately, of course, the goal will be to offer suggestions
that are consistent with all of the patient's values and
adaptive goals; for example, exercising regularly **and**
meeting one's important commitments, including of course
one's commitments to one's own psychological and physical
health.]*

**Patient: You can't exercise. So that's one piece I know about
for sure.**

*[The part of the patient that is ambivalent, at best, about
exercise continues to express itself. The utterances, offered by
the patient, can be viewed as self-suggestions that are likely
automatically cued whenever the idea of exercise comes up.
Here, that part is saying/suggesting, "You can't exercise." I
chose not to reflect this idea, which would strengthen it,
because I judged it to not be a particularly useful self-
suggestion. As discussed previously, it may not be possible to
erase self-suggestions that are already in place and are not
useful. However, it is possible to associate new ideas to
them—a kind of re-framing—so that they lose their negative
power, or even become self-suggestions that increase the
chances of positive behavior change. Although I did not do so
in this instance, I could have suggested an idea to associate
with this negative self-suggestions, "...all the time." So, for
example, I might have said, "Yes, you can't exercise **all the
time**." This is a truism that also implies the suggestion, "But
you can exercise some of the time."]*

**Patient continues: Um... let's see, once I start the exercise,
generally speaking, that's... that's fine, that's all I need to
do, is get on the bike, get my sneakers on, and get out the
door, or, whatever it is. The priming behaviors really hold**

for me. But it's getting from wherever I am, which is usually a state of stress and feeling overwhelmed, to this simple, "You need to do this, this is good for you, do it."

*[The tone used by the patient here—reflected by the tone that is not clearly communicated by the text alone, as well as by the choice of the word "need"—suggested to me that this was another example of "should"-type language that would likely interfere with success at achieving the goal. One useful response in this situation is to reflect a **portion** of what the patient said that is adaptive and consistent with the patient's stated goal: to carve out and nurture the most useful part of the patient's own self-suggestion. For example, in my response below.]*

MJ: You know, deep inside, that *exercise is good for you.*

[Reflections also help to keep the patient talking. The more the patient speaks during this preliminary open question and reflection stage, the more "already formed self-suggestions" will be put on the table for consideration. This makes it easier to: (1) identify the specific words to use in the suggestions during the formal hypnosis stage, (2) hear and understand (with the aim of utilizing) the most adaptive portions of existing self-suggestions, and (3) understand the (possibly conflicting) beliefs, goals, and values of all aspects of the patient—goals and values that might need to be reconciled in order to develop the most feasible plan.]

MJ continues: Mm-kay. And so, on average, in the last couple weeks, what's been the number of times per week?

[I made an error here. I asked a closed question instead of an open question. But the patient was very kind and continued as if I asked an open question. Not all patients are this helpful; this is a dream patient!]

Patient: Okay well, this is, this is good because I, when I travel, it's harder, because I don't have control over my time in certain ways. I have a certain schedule, and people expect me to adhere to the schedule and I expect me to adhere to the schedule.

MJ: Sure, you are *a responsible person* and *meet your commitments.*

Patient: So I would say, uh, it has been very irregular. There were... there were times when I was able to walk as part of what I was doing that day. In Vienna I went to the opera.

MJ: Mm-hmm.

Patient: And because of the traffic, we had to take the subway. That involved a lot of steps and a lot of walking, which was good, which was great.

MJ: Yeah. *Walking is good.*

Patient: But that doesn't always happen. You know, if it's not built in, then I have trouble. I usually convince myself I'm tired—this happened a number of times on a recent trip. "Oh, you're tired, you don't feel like exercising," and "You can do it tomorrow" and "What's the big deal?'

[More useful information about the self-suggestions that could potentially interfere with the goal of regular exercise. To the extent that these can be morphed into more useful suggestions by either carving out the most useful ideas, or associating useful ideas to them that are acceptable to the patient, they will be less likely to interfere in the future. A suggestion, for example, that associates the feeling of tiredness or fatigue with a desire to engage in exercise, because moderate exercise is an effective strategy for addressing acute fatigue. Or a suggestion that emphasizes

*the "**You can do it**" portion of the "You can do it tomorrow" idea, while also adding the additional idea, "... and today. Yes, **you can do it today** and tomorrow." Or a suggestion that "Yes, exercising regularly for my health is a valued goal." The point here is that the patient is providing important information that can be used to create suggestions that may be particularly effective for this specific patient. At this point during the demonstration, however, one of my goals was to explore with the patient what the most reasonable exercise goal for her would be, given what is most feasible in her life. The challenges of exercising regularly when traveling offered me an opportunity to broach this subject.]*

MJ: So, this goal of exercising daily. Does it make sense to have this goal when you travel as well? Or is it a different thing when you travel, do you think?

Patient: I think that when I travel, I need, in some ways I need to extend myself *more*.

[Okay. That didn't work. I'll have to come at this from another angle. But I am learning more about this patient and how she may be someone who expects a great deal from herself, and as a result may sometimes judge herself to come up short (and then perhaps feel guilty and discouraged; feelings that interfere with motivation). I will be keeping my ears open for ideas expressed by her and ideas that come to me that would offer acceptable alternatives to self-judging.]

MJ: I see.

Patient: Um, I don't think it's any *less* possible to exercise every day when I travel.

MJ: Okay.

Patient: Although I would say one thing. If I've had a long day and... and there's a dinner or something at the end of it, then I end up having to make a choice between sleep and exercise, and I usually choose sleep.

MJ: And as you think about it rationally, does that make sense?

[Here I am asking her to step back (engage in "slow thinking," cf. Kahneman, 2011) and make rational decisions about health behaviors consistent with all of her values and goals. For this type of discussion, Hypnotic Reflective Listening is similar to traditional cognitive therapy. Here, I wanted to invite her to explore the possibility that a conscious choice to not exercise is not an "excuse," and therefore nothing to feel guilty about.]

Patient: Yeah, I think it does.

MJ: *You want to make the right choices for you and your health.*

Patient: Uh-huh.

[So now I will have another go at exploring the possibility that she may not need to exercise every day as a viable goal. This time, I will use humor by reflecting the aspect of herself that has incredibly high standards.]

MJ: And so... I want to be sure I understand this. ... Is your goal to exercise seven days a week because your... you want to be perfect?

Patient: *[Laughter]* That sounds like me! *[Laughter]* Right, it does sound like me.

[Okay. Now we're on the right track.]

Patient continues: Although, I would say I believe that when I include movement every day of some kind I'm going to feel better.

[The "high standards" ego state of the patient wants to be sure that she is understood. Also, this ego state is absolutely correct in this instance. Some kind of movement every day — not necessarily 45 minutes of scheduled exercise activity — is reasonable, realistic, and consistent with the goal of remaining healthy. It is important to acknowledge this because it is more effective to have all ego states on board with the goal of exercising more. As will be seen, I respond by reflecting this idea. Also, even though we have not initiated formal hypnosis, we are already in "resonance," because we have been paying close attention to each other. So what I say has the potential to be understood deeply; to be accepted as a hypnotic suggestion. I therefore view what I say at this point to **be** *a hypnotic suggestion.]*

MJ: *[Speaking slowly and carefully, emphasizing the importance of the suggestion.]* **When you move... and exercise... you're going to feel better.**

Patient: Right.

[Suggestion accepted.]

Patient: I'm going to have more energy, for example.

[She is off and running. A very clear self-suggestion entirely consistent with her goal. She has said it herself so the idea already exists inside her. This self-suggestion is worth reflecting in order to strengthen and nurture it.]

MJ: *[Speaking carefully, emphasizing the importance of the suggestion.]* **When you move and exercise more, you're going to have more energy...**

[And now that "energy" has been mentioned by the patient as an outcome of exercise, this is also an opportunity to offer the suggestion that fatigue could be a cue for exercising.]

MJ continues: So when you say to yourself "I'm tired," that could be a cue that, "Ah! Now is the time to get out and do a little movement."

[Note also the idea of it being "a little movement." An idea consistent with what the patient said earlier about exercise is not being a "big deal," as well as the patient's comment that once she is primed, she continues. So starting with "a little movement" will likely result in 45 minutes of exercise.]

Patient: Right, right.

[She said "right" twice! A good sign. Perhaps she is communicating that she is very much accepting the suggestion. Or perhaps she is responding to the fact that I had offered two different suggestions, so she is saying she is accepting both of them.]

MJ: So "I'm tired" is no longer an excuse, *feeling tired is a cue, a cue that now would be a good time to exercise.*

[A solution and reframe. The goal here is to add suggestions that reframe the idea of "excuses," because the idea of "excuses" likely leads to guilt and therefore interferes with goal attainment.]

Patient: That's great! That sounds really great.

[Idea accepted.]

MJ: So, I'm wondering, and here I am talking to your rational self...

[Asking the patient to engage in "slow thinking" again here, as I am about to propose a goal different than what she stated

at first. I want to be respectful of the idea that she is in charge of the goal she wishes for herself. So I am inviting her to dissociate from any "automatic" (fast thinking) responses, and to think carefully about what is in her best interest overall.]

MJ continues: And I'm wondering... maybe you might want to shoot for five days a week, even if seven might be ideal.

Patient: Yes. Now that I think about this, that's right.

[That was almost too easy. I want to double check.]

MJ: That fits? That really does fit?

Patient: I think it really does.

MJ: Okay, and of course, a little movement every day, *feels so good.*

*[But I still acknowledge that at least "a little movement" every day is useful, and I re-state the suggestion linking movement/exercise to **feeling good**.]*

Patient: Right.

[She had mentioned earlier that she finds priming behaviors useful. So now we move on to utilizing this resource that already exists.]

MJ: Now, um, you said earlier that what helps you is actually just getting into the exercise clothes. Once it happens, it happens.

Patient: Yeah, it's true.

MJ: So a goal might be, not necessarily to exercise, but to simply just get ready to exercise, to just get into the clothes.

Patient: Right.

MJ: How does that sound?

Patient: I think that sounds right. And I can even say something like "...getting into my more *comfortable* clothes."

[She really is an ideal patient. Providing very nice text for hypnotic suggestions. Again, it is more effective to nurture ideas that are already there than to plant new ones.]

MJ: Nice.

Patient: Because they are, yeah.

MJ: Because doing things regularly and ritually helps build in habits, so you know, you probably brush your teeth every day.

[Utilizing teeth brushing as an example of how healthy behaviors can become easy and automatic.]

Patient: Yeah.

MJ: Probably at certain times.

Patient: Yes, I do.

MJ: And it's automatic, almost. If you didn't, it would feel uncomfortable. But brushing your teeth actually feels comfortable, and natural, and automatic...

Patient: Yes.

MJ: It's now an automatic response. *Well, exercising regularly can become an automatic thing, like brushing your teeth.*

Patient: Great. Great.

[I am enjoying how she communicates acceptance of an idea by repeating herself.]

MJ: *[What follows are stated as dry runs of hypnotic suggestions. I want to observe how she responds to the ideas, in order to determine whether or not they are viable suggestions to use during Phase 2]* It's something that you just do. ... It's part of what you *do* every day to maintain your health, to continue to do the good things you want to do in your life and just to feel better.

Patient: Yes.

> *[Suggestion accepted. The wording is viable as a potentially effective hypnotic suggestion.]*

MJ: Okay. And so... is there a certain time that might help with that? When might be a good time to automatically have an urge to exercise?

Patient: I think at the end of the day.

MJ: Okay.

Patient: Uh... at the end of my workday. That's really the junction that I can make work.

MJ: Got it.

Patient: Uh, occasionally, I will not have patients or anything scheduled in the morning and then that's easy. But I notice, I don't feel like exercising then.

I want to just... want to use the time, you know, differently. Have more freedom. But at the end of a workday, that's the time when I can sort of motivate myself a little better.

MJ: Yes. And in fact, you don't even have to motivate yourself. It will just be. *You will be motivated.*

Patient: Right. There you go.

[The affect and tone indicate that this idea is fully acceptable.]

MJ: And... and in particular... when you are tired, that's the cue... "*Now is a good time to exercise.*"

Patient: Ahh. Yes. Yes.

[The same general suggestion repeated. And again, the affect and tone indicate that this idea is acceptable. A list of useful suggestions is being developed.]

MJ: Right. ... End of the day, in your comfortable clothes. Now briefly what are... listing off... what are the good reasons to do this?

[Open question to elicit motivating factors to include in the suggestions during the formal hypnosis session.]

Patient: Oh my goodness! Uh, keep my weight at an optimal level. Which I mostly do.

I noticed I put on a few pounds while I was traveling, but I expect that. That's not a problem. I'll take that off in the next week. So that's number one.

MJ: Okay. Keeping your weight at an optimal level.

Patient: Number two, uh, I think that it moves me out of my head and into my body.

MJ: Yes. Out of your head and into your body.

Patient: So I am more expansive when I have been exercising. I also experience less stress. I can also have a terrible buildup of stress. Just an awful, awful day. And after I exercise, I don't have that stress anymore.

MJ: And so instead of the stress what do you feel?

[Asked in order to be able to identify useful wording for a positive suggestion; i.e., instead of suggesting, "... so you don't have that stress anymore," which would paradoxically suggest stress.]

Patient: Uhm, I feel... I would say calm.

MJ: Calm, OK.

Patient: I would feel uhm, what's the word? It's... it's... uhm... I feel like things are happening like the way they need to. ... If that makes sense. Sort of like, everything is, moving according to... in a good way for me.

MJ: Mm-hmm. Everything moving in a good way for you.

Patient: And it may take me a while to get there you know. Like I can have that thought.

[A self-suggestion for patience with herself. An idea that would likely be useful as an automatic thought for this patient. So worth reflecting to nurture and strengthen.]

MJ: Ya. You can be patient with yourself.

Patient: It's getting that thought and the feeling together.

MJ: And the feeling of calmness... the thought of everything moving together in a good way.

Patient: Ya.

MJ: *These thoughts and feelings can be a part of this experience of moving and exercising in these comfortable clothes...*

Patient: That's right. That's right.

MJ: OK. Any other reasons? Those are perfectly good reasons. Anything else that really stands out?

Patient: I think that's probably good… good enough. Those three. Ya.

Phase 2: Formal hypnotic session

MJ: Okay. So, what I would propose now is that, is that we just move into formal hypnosis… you go ahead and get yourself into a state and when you are ready to hear some ideas…

> *[This patient has a great deal of experience with hypnosis, and so she is able to enter a state of readiness on her own.]*

Just give your head a nod when you are ready… and then I'll talk with you for a little bit…

Patient: *[Sits quietly for about five seconds, and then nods.]*

MJ: OK. So, Catherine, *[Note: The name of the patient was changed in this transcript to maintain confidentiality.]* we've been talking some about your goals for your well-being and your health. … And in particular, your goal for having movement and exercise become more and more a part of your everyday experience.

Something that you do nearly every day, perhaps five times every week, and perhaps starting very soon. Experiencing a sense at the end of the workday that it is *now time to get into comfortable clothes.* Comfortable clothes for your health and your well-being.

A sense of inner motivation that *now is the time to move.* In particular in the *end of the workday* if you feel tired, this is a *particularly good time* to get into comfortable clothes… and then go and do whatever exercise or activity that is just right for you, right then.

Knowing that when you do this, and as you do this, you will feel more... calm. You'll have a deep sense that everything is moving in a good way. Knowing that this will help you meet your important health goals. To maintain an ideal weight. To maintain a sense of strength, and confidence.

And this urge to move is becoming... more and more... an automatic response at the end of the workday. There will just be this automatic urge... to get into these comfortable clothes. And as you do this, over time, it will more and more become automatic, just like brushing your teeth.

An automatic part of every day, maybe five days per week, or even more, if it is *right for you and your goals.*

And I expect that as you continue to do this, you'll find that your work will become even more efficient because you'll have the strength and energy to do the work that you'd like to do.

> *[A suggestion that was not specifically discussed, but meant to address the idea that she may not always feel like there is time for exercise. If exercise makes you more efficient, however, then exercising regularly will in fact give her more time, because of the greater efficiency. So, the suggestion offered here was informed by the previous discussion.]*

This will make your work become more effective, and impactful. By simply allowing yourself to be comfortable and move every day.

Now, in a moment I will be quiet. And when I am, Catherine, you can allow the eyes to open... when the *most important and useful* of these ideas are ready to sink into your mind.

[Giving Catherine the option of only accepting those ideas that are useful, in the event that the suggestion that was not specifically discussed, but that was offered, is not consistent with her goals.]

Sink in your unconscious and remain there *as long as they continue to be helpful*.

[A suggestion that may be useful now might end up being less useful at a different time in a person's life. Or it might be replaced by a similar but ultimately more useful suggestion in the future. Therefore, the patient is offered the post-hypnotic suggestion that the ideas offered will stay in place as long as, and only as long as, they continue to be helpful.]

Go ahead and allow yourself to come back when you are ready by allowing the eyes to open.

Patient: Mmmm. That was a nice break. Thank you.

MJ: You are very welcome, Catherine. Any final questions or comments?

Patient: I'm really looking forward to uh, I have to say, to the end of my workday today. *[Laughter]* And uh, I just, somehow I just feel lifted up.

MJ: Nice.

Patient: A little more optimistic.

MJ: A little more optimistic. Wonderful.

Patient: And like I'm anticipating something that's going to be good.

MJ: *Something good is going to happen*. And the whole quality of your life will improve a notch, for so many reasons.

Two-year follow-up:
Written by Catherine

I wrote to Catherine and invited her to review the chapter's transcript and requested her permission to present it here (permission was granted). She also suggested that it would be useful to describe her long-term response to the single session, and I agreed whole heartedly. Below is her response.

Mark, it's really enjoyable to review this experience with you. Two years later, the three suggestions we found are still useful:

1. At the end of my workday, it feels very important to get into comfortable clothes. I find myself looking forward to that change, and it is very rare after doing so that I don't ease into some type of movement or exercise.

2. The urge to move has become more natural and automatic.

3. I have a feeling of calm about exercise and body movement that whatever happens is what needs to happen, without pushing or scolding myself. In fact, it's really amazing to realize that I cannot recall a single instance when I did not engage in good exercise two days in a row—in other words, I have been able to self-correct. If I don't change into comfortable clothes and ease into some kind of movement that feels good at the end of my workday, I notice and want to do so the next day.

4. So this change has come about without challenging myself to accomplish this goal, a former approach to

exercise that was linked to stress. Instead, now I experience more *curiosity*—how will I feel this evening? Will I end up wanting to exercise? If I encounter resistance, I ask myself some version of the question, "What would make it easy for me to *want* to exercise or move my body so that I feel more energetic, more refreshed and alive?"

References

Anbar, R. D. (2008). Subconscious guided therapy with hypnosis. *American Journal of Clinical Hypnnosis, 50*, 323-334.

Bargh, J. A. (2014). Our unconscious mind. *Scientific American, 310*, 30-37.

Beck, A. T., & Dozois, D. J. (2011). Cognitive therapy: Current status and future directions. *Annual Review of Medicine, 62*, 397-409.

Beck, J. S. (2011). *Cognitive behavioral therapy: Basics and beyond* (2nd ed.). NewYork, NY: Guilford Press.

Bo, S., Rahimi, F., Goitre, I., Properzi, B., Ponzo, V., Regaldo, G., . . . Broglio, F. (2018). Effects of self-conditioning techniques (self-hypnosis) in promoting weight loss in patients with severe obesity: A randomized controlled trial. *Obesity, 26*, 1422-1429.

Entwistle, P. A., Webb, R. J., Abayomi, J. C., Johnson, B., Sparkes, A. C., & Davies, I. G. (2014). Unconscious agendas in the etiology of refractory obesity and the role of hypnosis in their identification and resolution: A new paradigm for weight-management programs or a paradigm revisited? *International Journal of Clinical and Experimental Hypnosis, 62*, 330-359.

Gilson, M., Freeman, A., Yates, M. J., & Freeman, S. M. (2009). *Overcoming depression: A cognitive therapy approach.* New York, NY: Oxford University Press.

Ginot, E. (2017). The enacted unconscious: A neuropsychological model of unconscious processes. *Annals of the New York Academy of Sciences, 1406,* 71-76.

Gordon, T. (1970). *Parent effectiveness training.* New York, NY: Wyden.

Green, J. P., & Lynn, S. J. (2000). Hypnosis and suggestion-based approaches to smoking cessation: An examination of the evidence. *International Journal of Clinical and Experimental Hypnosis, 48,* 195-224.

Green, J. P., & Lynn, S. J. (2017). A multifaceted hypnosis smoking-cessation program: Enhancing motivation and goal attainment. *International Journal of Clinical and Experimental Hypnosis, 65,* 308-335.

Hanrahan, F., Field, A. P., Jones, F. W., & Davey, G. C. (2013). A meta-analysis of cognitive therapy for worry in generalized anxiety disorder. *Clinical Psychology Review, 33,* 120-132.

Hofmann, S. G., Asmundson, G. J., & Beck, A. T. (2013). The science of cognitive therapy. *Behavior Therapy, 44,* 199-212.

Kahneman, D. (2011). *Thinking, fast and slow.* New York, NY: Farrar, Straus, and Giroux.

Kirsch, I., Montgomery, G., & Sapirstein, G. (1995). Hypnosis as an adjunct to cognitive-behavioral psychotherapy: A meta-analysis. *Journal of Consulting and Clinical Psychology, 63,* 214-220.

Landry, M., Appourchaux, K., & Raz, A. (2014). Elucidating unconscious processing with instrumental hypnosis. *Frontiers in Psychology, 5,* 785.

Lorenzo-Luaces, L., German, R. E., & DeRubeis, R. J. (2015). It's complicated: The relation between cognitive change procedures, cognitive change, and symptom change in cognitive therapy for depression. *Clinical Psychology Review, 41,* 3-15.

Mello, P. G., Silva, G. R., Donat, J. C., & Kristensen, C. H. (2013). An update on the efficacy of cognitive-behavioral therapy, cognitive therapy, and exposure therapy for posttraumatic stress disorder. *Internatitional Journal of Psychiatry in Medicine, 46,* 339-357.

Miller, W. R., & Rollnick, R. (2013). *Motivational interviewing: Helping people Change* (3rd ed.). New York, NY: Guilford Press.

Mott, T., Jr., & Roberts, J. (1979). Obesity and hypnosis: a review of the literature. *American Journal of Clinical Hypnosis, 22,* 3-7.

Roders, C. R. (1951). *Client-centered therapy.* Boston, MA: Houghton-Mifflin.

Zeig, J. K. (Ed.). (1994). *Ericksonian methods: The essence of the story.* New York, NY: Routledge.

CHAPTER 11

The Door Technique

Enayatollah Shahidi

When you understand how man really defends his intellectual ideas and how emotional he gets about it, you should realize that the first thing in psychotherapy is not to try to compel him to change his ideation; rather you go along with it and change it in a gradual fashion and create situations wherein he himself willingly changes his thinking.

—Milton H. Erickson

Enayatollah Shahidi, who goes by Enayat, is a physician who specializes in cognitive-behavioral psychotherapy. He resides in both Iran and Italy and is a well-recognized and popular Iranian therapist, author, translator, speaker, and workshop facilitator. In 1994, when he was an intern in a psychiatric hospital at Tehran University of Medical Sciences, he saw a poster of a hypnotherapy course in the hospital. He was immediately drawn to it and registered for the course. This is when his journey to practicing hypnosis began, and now it's something he cannot see himself living without, both professionally and personally. He has been practicing hypnotherapy since 1994 and has taught clinical hypnosis to professionals in Asia, North America, and Europe since 2001. In addition to the great therapists who were his teachers, he has been most influenced by Milton H. Erickson's books, Assen Alladin's books and workshops, and the books and workshops of Jeffrey Zeig. Based on his training and his own invaluable experiences, Enayat typically uses cognitive techniques, Ericksonian techniques, or a combination of both as his hypnotherapeutic approach. This varies depending on the patient's personality and therapeutic needs. Enayat has written two books and translated six books from either English or Italian into Persian. In collaboration with two close colleagues, Bernhard Trenkle and Mehdi Fathi, he co-organized several successful international congresses of hypnosis in Iran. Since 2012, he has been a faculty member at various international congresses on hypnosis. He has been a member of the Board of Directors of the Iranian Scientific Society of Clinical Hypnosis (ISSCH) since 2011, and he is currently the vice-president and treasurer of the society. He has also been a board member of the International Society of Hypnosis (ISH) since 2015 and was elected secretary/treasurer of the society for the 2018-2021 term.

*   *   *

Before I delve into my main subject and describe the Door Technique, I'd like to first touch upon the importance of the common elements that contribute to successful therapy and emphasize that the way a therapist implements therapeutic techniques is more important than the techniques themselves.

What are the key factors that impact the outcomes of various psychotherapies? How is it that diverse psycho-therapeutic approaches can all effectively treat a particular disorder, despite the fact that they have different theories about the etiology, different perspectives towards the problem, and use different therapeutic techniques? Is it the specific approach or the common factors that are most important?

Our understanding of the so-called common factors that underlie the efficacy of therapy has a long history in psychiatry, originating with a seminal article by Saul Rosenzweig in 1936 (Rosenzweig, 1936), then popularized by Jerome and Julia Frank in the various editions of their book *Persuasion and Healing* (e.g., Frank & Frank, 1993). Without going into too much detail, I would like to emphasize that for a therapy to be effective we need much more than good techniques. Among the various common factors that have been identified, I believe *interpersonal relationships, empathy, therapeutic alliance, goal consensus/ collaboration,* and *expectations* to be the most important.

In addition to the specific content of each technique and the above-mentioned common factors, what really determines the technique's effectiveness is the way it is implemented. According to Albert Mehrabian, when you talk face-to-face with someone, the way you speak (paralanguage) and the way you use your body language make up 93% of the message; while the content makes up the remaining 7% (Mehrabian, 1969). But what about a hypnotic session, during which the patient's eyes are often closed? One can easily assume that the body language would be of less significance and that a combination of content and paralanguage would be of greater importance.

Thus, in addition to the wording of suggestions, the way you use words; the prosody of your speech; how you create sound; the pauses, tone, intonation, accent, pitch, volume and speed of the speech are of paramount importance.

Pauses are a way of adding emphasis to words and phrases. Pauses also allow the patient to go internal and to do searches related to the word or phrase before the pause. Novice hypnotherapists frequently talk nonstop. Skilled use of pauses and other elements of speech are part of what differentiate expert hypnotherapists from beginners.

When you implement a hypnotherapeutic technique using a more empathic and persuading voice, it is much more influential. When you speak in a relaxing way, your patients tend to be relaxed, even if the words you use may not exactly match the treatment goal. I believe we can hypnotize people using a language that patients do not understand, just by using an appropriate paralanguage; much like a person might soothe a child even when the child does not yet understand the content of what is being said. This is exactly what happens to preverbal infants when listening to lullabies; they do not understand the meaning of the words, but they experience comfort nevertheless.

Let's go back to the discussion of hypnotic techniques. I believe every hypnotherapist should know and be able to use a variety of hypnotic techniques. In practice, however, it is likely that each clinician has a set of favorite or preferred techniques that he or she uses more often. Among the countless hypnotherapeutic techniques, I prefer those which are multipotent. Learning to use these techniques is cost effective! Their flexibility and multipotency make them effective for treating a wide range of presenting problems, and you can utilize them in various situations; an outstanding advantage for both beginners and experts.

In 2008, when I was reading the book *Handbook of Cognitive Hypnotherapy for Depression* (Alladin, 2007), I learned about an effective technique named The Door of Forgiveness, devised by Helen Watkins. The book was written by Assen Alladin, a brilliant friend of mine who unfortunately passed away in 2017. With this technique, patients are asked to imagine walking down a corridor, at the end of which there is a big door named the Door of Forgiveness. Passing through the door is a sign that the patients have successfully forgiven themselves or other important people of their life.

While walking down the corridor, patients notice several doors on either side of the corridor that they must pass before reaching the Door of Forgiveness. Some of these doors may appear familiar or meaningful, and some may not. Patients are encouraged to open each meaningful door and describe to the therapist what he or she observes in the room beyond the door. The idea is for the patient to resolve any experience or relationship from the past that may be associated with or causing guilt before reaching the Door of Forgiveness.

Patients cannot go through the Door of Forgiveness until they have passed all the meaningful side doors and have dealt with the issues, events, or memories that lie beyond each of these doors. Often, when a patient opens a door an emotional abreaction occurs. Importantly, the therapist does not provide any interpretation and does not act as the forgiver. The therapist's role is to provide direction and support.

Some people have very vivid images during this technique. Take Romina, for example. She is a 19-year-old artist who experienced this technique, facilitated by me. When I told her that I planned to write a chapter on the Door Technique, she expressed a desire to draw an illustration of her hypnotic visualization and gave me consent to include it in this book. Thanks to Romina's creation, you can see how one may feel dissociated during this technique (see Figure 11.1). The main part of the illustration depicts walking towards the final door, while other parts are visiting the side rooms.

I have found this method to be very useful and have developed it further into a multipotent technique. I use the Door Technique not only as the Door of Forgiveness but also as the Door of Success, the Door of Happiness, the Door of Health, the Door of Calmness, the Door of Freedom, the Door of Beauty, and so on. As when using the Door of Forgiveness, for each of these "doors," patients are asked to experience themselves as walking down a corridor with multiple side doors. I have noticed that it is possible to integrate this approach with other techniques and develop them to be used not only as hypnotherapeutic techniques but also as induction and deepening techniques.

This is why I usually ask patients to close their eyes, take a few deep breaths, and focus on their breaths and on the subtle feelings associated with each breath. They are encouraged to feel the mild freshness of the air passing through their nose, the expansion of their chest, and the stretching out of the intercostal muscles each time they inhale. They can feel the air passing through their nose, mouth, throat, and the airway passages down into their lungs, where the air enters small chambers called alveoli that have semitransparent walls. The patients are told that they can imagine travelling deep into the lungs like a molecule of oxygen and can pass through the walls of the alveoli and surrounding capillaries to enter small arteries. By this time, the patient is often well hypnotized, and we can deepen the experience by providing more details.

The patient is then asked to imagine him/herself as an oxygen molecule riding on a red blood cell as a vehicle, surfing in the blood vessels all throughout the body.

As I have already mentioned, I love multipotent techniques. So, at this point you, as the clinician, can decide to guide the patient into a muscle to be relaxed, a painful area to be relieved, a body organ to work more efficiently, the labyrinths of brain and mind to experience the Door Technique, or another part of the body for a different therapeutic goal.

Figure 11.1. Patient's illustration of her visualization during the Door Technique.

It is the patient's unconscious mind that decides which doors are important and which ones are not. In a lot of cases, the patient is astonished to see that their unconscious choices are different from those of the conscious mind.

The Door Technique Transcript

[We invite patients to choose among a few induction techniques.]

Clinician: There are a lot of ways to start a pleasant hypnotic session. Typically, people start their hypnotic session in a way that is most comfortable for them.

[While patients are asked to choose their preferred way of entering a hypnotic state, we actually provide them with the illusion of choice.]

Some people sit back, breathe deeply, and let their bodies relax with each breath.

Others prefer to close their eyes and imagine themselves safely floating on gentle waves in an open body of water. And you may choose either of these or create your own way of entering a pleasant hypnotic state. So just sit back... relax, close your eyes, and get as comfortable as you want.

[As you see, there is no real difference between the various options. Patients often create their own preferred combination of choices.]

You may like to imagine yourself in a safe, pleasant, and calming situation, while focusing on each relaxing breath... and the feelings associated with it.

[By well-illustrated, clearly described, effective multisensory descriptors, we invite patients to an inward absorption and let them go into a deeper hypnotic state.]

Allow your body to feel how pleasant it is to sense the mild freshness of the air on your face... feel the expansion of the chest when you deeply breathe in... and sense the lightness you feel when you breathe out.

Feel how relaxing it is that each time you exhale, any tension you once felt leaves your body... leaves your mind... the body feeling at ease and calm.

[Providing more details to facilitate the therapeutic process.]

As you breathe in and out, the air passes through your nose, mouth, and throat, down into your lungs, and you may want to accompany it. ... Is this not amazing to feel like a light molecule of oxygen that travels deep into the lungs and through to the alveoli? It's even more interesting to envision yourself passing through the semitransparent walls of the alveoli and the surrounding capillaries... to enter small arteries where you ride on red blood cells, surfing through blood vessels and entering into the labyrinths of the brain and the mind.

[The therapist describes imaginary corridors with side doors and then ultimately exit doors. This serves as an appropriate framework within which the therapy happens.]

I don't know if you know the hypnotic mind model. A model that helps you imagine what your mind looks like. ... A space full of corridors with numerous side doors. ... Each corridor is the pathway to a distinct goal and eventually ends at a beautiful bright door.

There are pathways and doors of forgiveness... happiness... success... health... love... and anything else that you may need to feel happier. ... You may or may not know that passing through each of the final doors results in relieving any negative emotions or tension you once felt about the subject and lets you feel free. ... Each door leads you to a better world... free from useless tension.

It's the time for you to utilize this exceptional opportunity to feel better... happier. ... You do not need to listen to me. ... Just imagine yourself walking through the corridor, leading you towards the Door of Forgiveness.

[Using confusional suggestions helps patients be more involved with the therapeutic process.]

I wonder if you have noticed that your mind is dissociated into several parts. ... One part of it listens to each word I say. ... Another part pays attention to the overall meaning... the other walks you through the corridor... and one part thinks about everything it wants.

There is even a part of your mind that does not think about anything. ... And you do not even need to listen to me. ... I am addressing your unconscious mind and you may let your conscious mind hover whenever it wants. ... Your unconscious mind is carefully following me even if your conscious mind is not aware of this. ... As a matter of fact, your conscious and unconscious minds are dissociated, and this is why hypnosis is so powerful.

[We then go back to the technique and guide the patient's concern towards the experiences in which forgiveness is the goal of the treatment.]

Just walk down the corridor and take a look at the side doors. ... Everybody has a collection of memories and experiences. ... Some of them are pleasant, while others are not. ... Either positive or negative, memories are so useful because we can learn from them without even trying.

Sometimes in the past we might have been hurt by another individual or even by our own actions. ... Remember how you used to find yourself thinking about these experiences over and over... and now notice your preference to set them aside and enjoy a pleasant feeling of freedom.

[By adding appropriate pauses and intonation, give your patients the opportunity to go deeper in the trance state and to do their own work in the cooperative endeavor of therapy.]

Have you ever thought about the amount of energy you devote to your unresolved issues? Are you going to continue wasting energy on such issues or do you want to redirect that energy towards success, happiness, and calmness? And you can use any of your conscious and unconscious resources that are appropriate to resolve the issues.

Maybe there are people that you need to forgive. ... Or maybe you need to forgive your own self. ... To take advantage of this outstanding opportunity you don't need to listen to me, just walk slowly down the corridor, towards the Door of Forgiveness.

You know that passing through the Door of Forgiveness results in you having forgiven yourself or any other individuals that you need to forgive to set yourself free.

[Help the patient find what is most relevant to their current situation by providing more details.]

Continue walking down the corridor under the dim light and take a look at the side doors. ... Some of these doors may appear familiar or meaningful to you, some of them may not.

And you won't go through the final Door of Forgiveness until you have successfully passed all the meaningful side doors and have let the unconscious mind deal with any issues, events, or memories. ... Memories are so useful because they are ours... and they are subjective, so they can be changed to let us feel free and happy.

Each door opens into a room that may be related to your current issue. ... Above each door you see a colored light. The colors signify the importance of each door and identifies which ones requires your attention. ... Maybe they are green, yellow, red, or any other color.

Some of these doors signal that they need to be opened. ... The signal could resemble a blinking light, a light that is kept on, a particular color with a specific meaning for you, or any other means that your unconscious mind recognizes.

Walk through the corridor and open the first meaningful side door... enter the room and observe what you see. ... Most likely, a colorful light has filled the room, maybe the same color as the light above the door. ... Just observe what you see, and you will find out what the issue, memory, or event is that is associated with this room.

Is it about someone you know?

Is it about an event?

Is it about yourself?

> [After finding out the issue beyond each door, we switch into therapeutic techniques. Often, when a patient enters a door an emotional abreaction occurs. It is important to note that the therapist does not interpret this. Nor does the therapist act as the forgiver. The therapist's role is to provide direction and support.]

Perhaps you would like to discuss what you see, or just watch and let your unconscious mind decide what to do. ... Your unconscious mind is a reliable reservoir of solutions.

Trust your unconscious mind and let it choose what you need most in order to deal with the situation. ... You don't need to *pay special attention to me*, you just need to watch what you see and let your unconscious mind guide you through the process. ... In each situation, you may need to do something... you may need to forgive somebody... you may need to forgive yourself... or you may just need to let it go. ... It's your unconscious mind that chooses the best option.

And by your unconscious choice, you see that events and relationships from the past which caused you pain or any other negative emotion begin to resolve. ... As it resolves, the color the room is filled with and the color of the door light will gradually change into other colors. ... This is a sign for you and me that the issue is resolved, and you are ready to exit the room.

That's right! Very good!

Changing the color into green, blue, white or any other relaxing color makes you feel calm and free. ... After safely exiting the room you pass through another door to repeat the process of observing inside the room... letting the unconscious mind resolve the issue... letting the color change... sensing a feeling of freedom and passing through another room.

I don't know how many rooms you should visit before passing through the Door of Forgiveness, but I do know that *your* unconscious mind knows.

[We then prepare patients for successful termination of the trance. I often use permissive suggestions both to respect the feeling of self-control and to ensure that the unconscious mind has the required time to accomplish the therapeutic process.]

I also don't know when you will successfully accomplish the mission and go through the Door of Forgiveness... maybe in this session or in the next one. ... I just know that you will do it soon and at the best time for you. ... This will be the beginning of a new era in your life.

I really congratulate you. ... You are successfully setting your mind free to utilize all your potential, intelligence, and energy for your own happiness, calmness, and success.

Congratulations!

Did you understand all of what happened to you? Do you know how much you will be changing? Are you aware, now, of how useful being in a trance has been to you?

So, in a moment, I will be silent and let your wise unconscious mind lead you through the process. ... You may continue visiting the side rooms until successfully passing through the Door of Forgiveness, or you may go through it right now.... I don't know exactly when you will open your eyes, but I know that your unconscious mind knows this and will manage to let your eyes open soon. ... Let your eyes open into a new world in which you are the owner of your thoughts, your emotions, and your happiness.

Your unconscious mind will soon let your eyes be opened to come back here and now, fully alert.

Very good!

Just go ahead and let the unconscious mind manage to let your eyes be opened to come back here and now; fully alert, relieved, and free.

So, I will now be silent and wait for that moment.

References

Alladin, A. (2007). *Handbook of cognitive hypnotherapy for depression: An evidence-based approach.* Philadelphia, PA: Lippincott Williams & Wilkins.

Frank, J. D., & Frank, J. B. (1993). *Persuasion and healing: A comparative study of psychotherapy.* Baltimore, MD: Johns Hopkins University Press.

Mehrabian, A. (1969). Significance of posture and position in the communication of attitude and status relationships. *Psychological Bulletin, 71,* 359-372.

Rosenzweig, S. (1936). Some implicit common factors in diverse methods of psychotherapy. *American Journal of Orthopsychiatry 6,* 412-415.

For Further Reading...

Battino, R., & South, T. L. (2005). *Ericksonian approaches: A comparative manual.* Carmarthen, UK: Crown House Publishing.

Zeig, J. (2014). *The Induction of hypnosis: An Ericksonian elicitation approach.* Phoenix, AZ: Milton H. Erickson Foundation Press.

CHAPTER 12

Remembering Well-Being:
The U-Assessment and
Therapeutic Protocol

Dorothea Thomaßen

Dorothea Thomaßen is trained as a general surgeon. She has two additional areas of expertise: Traditional Chinese Medicine and Ericksonian hypnosis. She is a trainer and supervisor for the German Society for Dental Hypnosis and is the editor-in-chief of the German Journal of Dental Hypnosis. *She also teaches for the German Milton H. Erickson Society, facilitating seminars on pain management, changing habits, and hypno-oncology. At the present time, she has a private practice in Frankfurt am Main, Germany, where she works with patients of all ages, treating a variety of psychosomatic and somato-psychic disorders.*

* * *

The consequences of a surgeon's decisions are often far reaching. Imagine a patient with severe abdominal pain. With this patient, you first have to make a diagnosis, selecting from a number of different possibilities. The treatment(s) that are appropriate for one cause of the pain could be completely inappropriate for a different cause. For some conditions, one should operate immediately. In other cases, such as with severe infection, an operation would weaken the body. Then there are patients with so-called functional pain. For such patients, every organ is healthy, yet they still experience significant (and very real) pain. Finally, although rare, there are patients who pretend to have severe pain in order to avoid doing something they do not want to do, or to receive something that they think they cannot obtain in an easier way.

What these patients say during an evaluation may be very similar. But how their body responds during the examination, how their body smells, what their overall appearance is, the sound of their voice, what you hear when listening with the stethoscope; all of these factors differ from one patient to another and from one diagnosis to another.

With experience, a clinician learns to trust his or her own senses. Not only should the clinician listen carefully to the patient, but he or she should also be able to put the patient's words and the nonverbal and para-verbal signals into perspective. The more experience I have gained, the more I trust in nonverbal body signals as critical components of the assessment. As a result, my evaluations have become more accurate.

After having made the diagnosis and seeing how the patient responds to treatment, all the psychological changes that are occurring along with the physical healing can be observed. Based on my clinical experiences, my hypnotherapeutic thinking has become increasingly oriented towards state-dependent memory and state-dependent learning. This means that the patient's presenting problem and condition have a strong impact on his or her memory functions and shape what the patient is able to learn.

Up to this point, I have described the circumstances of an acute problem, in which the U-protocol (described later in this chapter) is not appropriate. In acute situations—new onset illness or injury—the patient has not yet had the opportunity to develop learned associations to the symptoms of the illness or injury. The U-protocol is most useful to address the suffering associated with chronic conditions.

The U-Assessment and Therapeutic Protocol (UATP) was first developed for treating patients who have chronic functional pain conditions such as migraine and bruxism, as well as patients with pain associated with autoimmune diseases or cancer. Even if there is an identifiable somatic cause for the pain, and particularly in patients with autoimmune diseases or cancer, there may also be a pain memory problem. In this case it would be possible to ease the suffering by erasing the stored pain memories; this is done by inviting patients to recall, and be reminded of, memories of well-being.

These days, I find it useful to use the UATP in every case where state-dependent memory might have an influence on the patient's symptoms. As it turns out, this is the condition in almost every case where patients have established a problematic response pattern. I also use the UATP for identifying treatment goals. For example, to identify patients who have phobias such as a fear of flying. The therapeutic goal in this case would of course be for the patient to be able to fly in a state of comfort and well-being.

But what does well-being feel like? Our body contains nerves that send information to the brain, which the brain then uses to create our experience. We have nerves from the top of the head to the soles of the feet, from the surface of our body (skin) to deep inside (bones). Interestingly, when we are healthy, we tend to be unaware of our body. The body is a medium that essentially becomes unconscious when it is working well. Normal proprioception is like a background; a stage for the senses of sight, hearing, smell, and taste, which are all concentrated at the head, combined with the kinesthetic structures in our ears that give us a sense of balance. Even more—these other senses are embedded in the sense of feeling. Eyelashes, a sensitive cornea, hairs in the nostrils, a tongue with a sense of touch—all serve to guard and protect the senses. As the body is a homeostatic self-adjusting intelligence, it does not usually need our conscious awareness to function well. We can observe our body processes, but we cannot usually control them directly. This is fine, of course, as it frees our consciousness to focus on our goals or otherwise enjoy our experiences.

One of my patients was a woman with a hemifacial spasm. The right side of her face quivered uncontrollably. She had a very difficult time seeing with both eyes. Reading was tiring, and she had a lot of headaches. When she tried to control her facial expression, her whole body became tense.

Because her primary symptom was so visible, she felt ashamed and led a life of seclusion. When I asked her what she wanted to achieve with treatment, she answered: "This [pointing to the right side of her face] should be gone!" I replied, "Do you really want half of your face to be gone?" "Of course not, I would only like the quivering to go away," she said. "And how would your face be then?" I asked. Taking a deep breath, she responded, "Then I would be happy." At that moment, her face distorted even more. Up to this point, she only described what should *not* be there, but not how she wanted her face to be. In order to identify a treatment goal to focus on, we needed a positive definition of healthy body sensations.

Very often patients say: "My body should do what I want. I don't want to have to think about it. This is annoying." To become healthy and to be able to forget about the body is a healthy response to normal self-regulation, as already mentioned. On the other hand, discomfort immediately attracts our attention and therefore limits what we are able to remember and learn. The steps required to move from illness and discomfort to wellness and well-being are often too many and too challenging for patients to take on their own.

However, when we are ill, we are motivated to move to wellness. Hypnosis makes it possible to achieve this goal through changing the focus of awareness. The UATP aims to provide a positive description of healthy proprioception. To achieve this goal, I follow the focus of the client, who usually begins treatment being absorbed by and focusing on the problem.

With the UATP, I first ask the patient to describe his or her experience associated with the illness. These qualities are written down on the left side of a flipchart in red (see Figure 12.1). In response, patients usually begin by describing or labelling the most bothersome symptoms. As they continue, and towards the end of their list of experiences, they will tend to describe the more discrete, almost normal sensations. After all symptoms are described, we then identify complementary positive or beneficial labels (i.e., what the patient would like to experience instead), which are written on the right side of the flipchart in green. To keep the steps simple, when identifying the positive responses I usually start in the reverse order of the red side, from the bottom to the top (see Figure 12.1). Because the symptoms at the end of the list are less troublesome, it is easier to find their antonyms.

Problem   Aim

A_P A_A

B_P **What** B_A

C_P **instead?** C_A

D_P D_A

E_P E_A

F_P F_A

G_P G_A

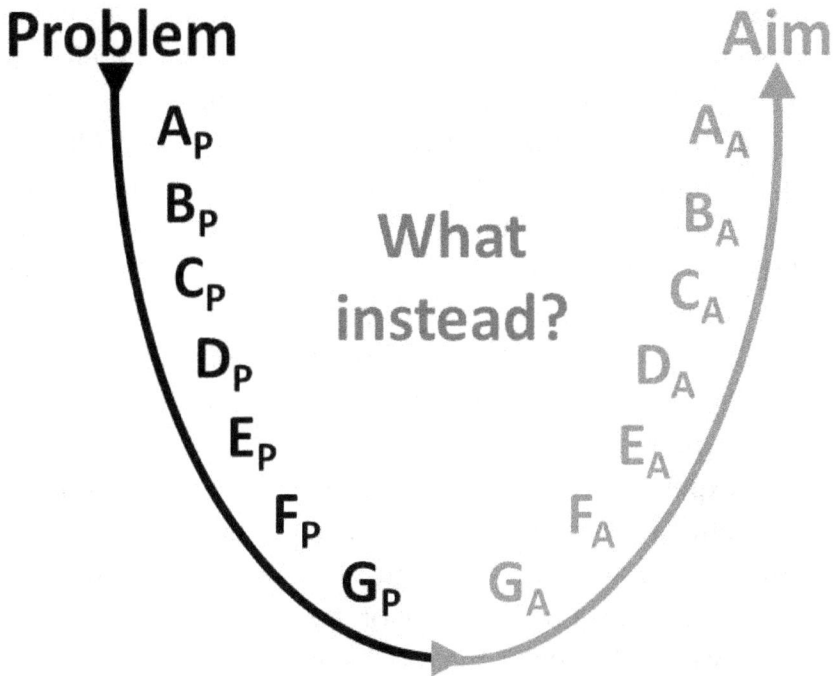

Figure 12.1. The U-Assessment and Therapeutic Protocol.

Because the patient has often been focusing on the negative symptoms for so long, he or she may have difficulty identifying the positive experience associated with each of the negative symptoms or experiences at first. However, as each positive quality is identified, it makes it easier to find the next. As with syphons, as soon as suction starts, water begins to easily flow upwards. The descending red list and ascending green list reciprocate with one another and form a U-shape.

Through visualization, patients learn to describe healthy feelings in their own words and to label them. Labelling also involves a process of remembering, given that patients have almost always, if not always, had the positive experiences in the past. Thus, the UATP is a 3-in-1 process: (1) a positive affect-bridge to comfort, (2) a process of activating favorable somatic feelings in the present, and (3) a process of future goal setting. Moreover, the process of seeing the symptoms and experiences on a flipchart and of naming and remembering somatic states involves the three senses of seeing, hearing, and feeling. One can often see, quite quickly, the beneficial impact of the process reflected in the faces of patients. They look satisfied as they scan the list; they nod and take deep breaths. The use of the flipchart is a key component of the whole therapy.

I would like to emphasize a few more points. First, many patients with somatic discomfort try to avoid describing those somatic experiences. When I asked my patient to describe her somatic experiences, she did not start with body sensations but with emotional reactions: "I get nervous. It is enough to drive me up the wall and to go through the roof." Interestingly, the house is often used as a metaphor for the body by patients: "Up the wall and through the roof" symbolizes a wish to leave the body. Second, patients also often describe their strategies for coping with the symptoms. In the case of the patient presenting with hemifacial spasm, she said, "I feel ashamed, so I live by myself"; she avoided social activities. Another coping strategy often described by my patients presenting with somatic symptoms is, "Ignore it and go on"; a dissociation tactic that suppresses the awareness of proprioception.

The word *proprioception* is composed of two components: *proprio* (i.e., one's own) and *ception* (i.e., to take or grasp). So proprioception makes our body our property. Very often, I find it paradoxical that pain memory and dissociation coexist with the experience of proprioception. It usually requires effort to focus on, explore, and "make one's own" disturbing somatic sensations, because reactions and coping strategies are not proprioceptive qualities. Importantly, as long as sensations are avoided, one cannot create a therapeutic alliance with a kinesthetic goal.

Whenever you focus on pain, there is awareness of the body in the here and now. My patient experienced sensations of cramping, tension, and pressure. Observing only one quality, such as pressure, makes the other sensations take a back seat. At the same time, pressure is only a part of the entire experience, and its intensity therefore is less than the whole complex of pain. As a result, the exploration and focus on discrete components of the entire experience increases the sense of self; often discomfort eases during this process. This makes it easier for patients to open their awareness to other (perhaps more comforting) body regions.

I asked in this case, "What does your neck feel like? How is your abdomen?" The patient had not yet noticed that her body was rigid, her hands were restless, and her feet were cold; that there was heat around her eyes and there were many other symptoms. Finally, I asked her to concentrate on her whole body and to be aware of every sensation at the same time. At this point, after the exploration of the individual components of their experience, even patients with chronic pain may say, "Right now, everything is ok," despite the fact that we continuously focused on the problem. *Focusing on and being more aware of somatic sensations makes it possible to integrate these sensations; to make them (again) one's own.* The process addresses dissociation and can facilitate homeostatic regulation, a process very well known in mindfulness training, which has become a standard tool in chronic pain management.

Once "everything is ok," it is easier to begin to explore the healthy, normal states and label them more precisely. But even when this is not possible at this stage in therapy, the long list of red (less than helpful) words describing symptoms is useful. These words form the basis for identifying the (more helpful) antonyms, which represent a path forward towards comfort and health. As a result, the more red words there are, the more green words we will identify.

The process of coming up with the green words requires the patient to comb through his or her experiences, looking for antonyms describing well-being. In this way, they start to activate these positive states. The body is able to identify wished-for states through remembering, and the positive somatic experiences identified become visible. One can observe how patients show small movements towards well-being as their awareness goes from one positive experience to another; their physiology changes. The terms "re-membering" and "re-minding" express it well. Words anchor states. What has been unconscious before becomes conscious and available. A memory of health is reinstalled, step-by-step.

Two points are crucial for the process to be effective. First, the word for the goal must be positive, without negation. Whenever there is a "not," clinicians are encouraged to ask, "What instead?" Still, many hidden denials can be missed; *painless, untroubled, unburdened, stress-free,* and *not tight* still contain the words *pain, trouble, burden, stress,* and *tight.* As long the patient works with a prefix or a suffix as *–less, un-, -free,* or *not,* I continue to ask, "… and what instead?"

This process increases access to a language of well-being. If the patient stops talking in terms of being *painless,* but instead in terms of having *comfort* and being at *ease;* if instead of being *untroubled* they identify a goal of feeling *safe* and *sound;* if they replace *unburdened* with *free* and *flexible; stress-free* is substituted by *relaxation* and *stability;* and *not tight* with *soft* and *easy going;* they will begin the process of feeling better. Especially, and importantly, if the replacement/goal labels are labels that they themselves identified.

The process can take time; the activation of the state comes first, naming it comes afterwards. If clinicians try to help with their own words and labels, they interfere with this intermediate step. It is the clinician's job to ask the right questions, not to find the answers. Thus, they should elicit the new labels from the clients, and then repeat back to the patient any positive antonyms that the patient mentions. When I demonstrate the technique in a seminar and reiterate all the green words of the list before going to the next step, the participants sometimes get annoyed ("We've already heard the words, why are you repeating them? Let's get on with it!"). However, when I ask the patient about the utility of hearing their own labels repeated back to them, they always find it helpful.

The second point I would like to emphasize is that the word for the problem and the word for the solution must belong to the same sensory domain. Of course, it would be *great* to be without pain, but *great* is a judgement, not a sensation. When my patient with hemifacial spasm said that she would be happy without these symptoms, I understood her very well. However, she mentioned an emotion, not a sensation; and her face distorted and deformed even more. Why was the presenting symptom getting worse instead of better? She spoke about herself, not about her body. Also, with other patients I have observed that often the expression of a wish, such as to be handsome and fit, is followed by a somatic aggravation. I believe that if patients focus on a picture, an ideal, on how they *should* be, that this elicits the opposite experience. This then causes stress, because they are rejecting the way they are now. The process of formulating their goal through the UATP has a more useful outcome. Through the process of state-remembering, they gain access to the state that they wish to experience; they start to experience their wish as a real possibility. However, when there is focus on an ideal, global sense of well-being as a goal for addressing a specific negative somatic sensation, this can contribute to ignoring the body's feedback, which may then lead to an increase in the symptoms. As a matter of fact, ignoring the body's feedback in an ongoing manner often leads to dis-ease.

When the patient has difficulty finding positive somatic words, it can help to focus on body parts that have healthy regulation. For example, after we had listed all symptoms, the patient with the hemispasm was not able to find proprioceptive antonyms for all of the symptoms. As the hemispasm afflicted only one side of her face, I asked her to be aware of and experience the other side, which was in good physical shape. She described it as "soft, peaceful, relaxed, with modulated temperature, elastic and flexible, familiar and at ease." As she did this, her whole face became calm and relaxed. It was obvious that the equivalent verbal properties gave rise to beneficial results. While she was scanning from one side to the other and back again, her eyes were moving as in Eye Movement Desensitization and Reprocessing (EMDR), she engaged in proprioceptive-induced reprocessing spontaneously.

The UATP can be used for a variety of presenting problems. Mental conflicts are usually accompanied by somatic configurations. For the protocol, the patients investigate their bodies while they imagine themselves having the problem. They become aware of how they dissociate as a way to cope with the symptoms. The felt sense of the dissociation is a link to the body. After patients have completed the whole process, they imagine themselves in the same situation feeling comfortable again; in this way they get access to resources which they have not been aware of previously. That is state-dependent memory and learning.

As I said in the beginning, the protocol is not appropriate for treating an acute injury or illness. Acute conditions have a strong impact on the mind; the UATP shows the power of words and language on somatic affects and effects. In acute situations, the clinician's responsibility also includes use of language. As words anchor states, salutogenic language is an important component of a well-stocked first aid kit. Often, clinicians have the same problem as patients with chronic pain; a biomedical focus and language focused on pathology. The medical language is full of positive language associated with negative results; i.e., "The patient tested positive for HIV...." In what way is an HIV infection positive? Medical language is full of less-than-useful words that begin with *de-* or *un-*, or end with *-free* and *-less*. Professionals need to learn to describe the outcome of their work in a language which leads to an open and healthy perspective.

The UATP does not work against the pattern; instead, symptoms are used as a resource to identify more useful experiences and to bring back awareness to body sensations. The end goal of comfort and well-being evolves through an investigation of the problem. It has many beneficial effects. Patients associate again with their bodies and they remember the sensations as a resource. They regain access to healthy sensations, activate positive self-regulation, and find their own salutogenic language.

When the patient's words are written down on a flipchart/poster, the poster becomes a constant visual companion. Many patients take a photo of their flipchart, others write the words down to take them home. I keep the flipchart/poster. In some cases, the UATP works as a single-session intervention; if not, I present the poster in following sessions as a reminder of the patient's goals and path towards wellness. Only if the goal changes, or if the same patient comes for a different reason at another time, we would go through a new protocol.

The patient's own words can be used by the patient and the therapist. These words not only provide a frame of reference but also a tool for the treatment. I also use the helpful/healing words identified by the patient in other communications with the patient and independent from the UATP. For example, I may incorporate them as suggestions during formal hypnosis sessions or when I am providing acupuncture or medication treatment. These words anchor states and bring back recollections of well-being.

Example Transcript

I have described the principles of the UATP with chronic pain memory. Now I want to provide an example of how to work with state-dependent memory and learning using behavioral patterns which have been established in the past. In this example, a colleague comes for supervision with a patient's health record. It is the first supervision.

Supervisor: What is your goal for the supervision?

Client: I want to understand myself better. Sometimes something jumps up at me. [She holds her right hand in front of her chest and moves it quickly upwards to her right side.] **And then I take it with me. I want to learn to handle it.**

Supervisor: What jumps up at you?

Client: It surrounds me like a cloud. It runs like a thread through my everyday life. I really take it with me. [With her hands she paints a cloud around herself, beginning at the top of her head.]

Supervisor: Let us investigate your experience a little bit closer. Here I have a flipchart. Please describe precisely, what happens to you, when something jumps up at you and the cloud comes into being. I will list what you tell me about your experience here. [Pointing to the flipchart.] **From**

this list we will come up with ideas for helping you to handle the situation later on, okay?

Client: *[Nods.]*

Supervisor: You said something jumps at you, surrounds you like a cloud and then it runs like a thread through your everyday life..."

> *[The supervisor writes on the flipchart in red: "Something jumps at me" (P1), "Cloud" (P2), and "It runs like a thread through my everyday life" (P3).]*

Client: Yes, and in my head I have a voice. It says continuously, "Be careful, do it right!" (P4)

Supervisor: What does it feel like to have this voice in your head?

Client: At the back of my head I have a disagreeable tingling (P5), and my forehead is tense (P6). ... Yes, that really blocks me (P7). ... Suddenly I feel obstructed (8P). *[She frowns.]*

Supervisor: When you are inside the cloud and this voice is talking in your head, the back of your head is tingling and the forehead is tense, what else is happening inside your body?

Client: I start trembling (P9), I get tense (P10) and agitated (P11). *[She wags her hands excitedly.]*

Supervisor: *[Pacing her movements.]* And how are your hands then?

Client: Sweaty and cold (P12), my whole body feels hot and cold (P13).

PROBLEM	AIM
1 Something jumps up at me	I have a protective cover and feel secure
2 Cloud	The cloud is floating above the patient and is small
3 It runs like a thread through my everyday life	I can leave it with the patient
4 In my head: be careful, do it right	I have everything
5 Back of the head disagreeable tingling	Harmonious, relaxed
6 Tension in the forehead	Open agreeable good feeling
7 Blockade	Confident, I am capable
8 Obstruction	I can engage with what is coming up
9 Trembling	Open and calm
10 Tension	Stable, balanced
11 Agitation	Centered and concentrating on what is happening, appropriately activated
12 Sweaty, cold hands	Nicely warm and dry
13 Hot and cold feeling in body	Comfortably warm
14 Breathing flat and staccato	Steady, rhythmic, deep, soft
15 Faint belly	Round, comfortable, calm
16 Dry throat	Humid
17 Voice high, artificial	Soft, empathic, calm
18 Thick voice	Authentic, certain, sure
19 Beating heart	Peaceful and calm
20 Tight movements	At ease, connected, congruent
21 Stand at attention	Wait and see, guarded, reclined, observing
22 Ready to jump	Reclined, looking from inside
23 Thigh tense	Released, soft, down to earth, relaxed
24 Standing beside myself	Centered, being one
25 Observing myself from the right side	Seeing the other person
26 Toes rolled inside, cramping	Grounded, soft, firm
27 Feet icy-cold	Warm, distinct feeling
28 Back and neck stiff	Mobile, flexible, composed

Figure 12.2. Example of a completed U-Assessment and Therapeutic Protocol flipchart.

Supervisor: When you are agitated and you feel hot, cold, and tense, what else is happening?

Client: Oh, my breathing gets flat and staccato (P14). I have a faint feeling in my belly (P15). *[She moves one hand upon her abdomen and one at her throat.]*

Supervisor: *[Also moving one hand to her throat.]* And how is it here?

Client: My throat is dry (P16) and yes, my voice gets high and artificial (P17), it is even thick (P18).

Supervisor: Anything else?

Client: My heart is beating (P19) and my movements are tight (P20). I stand-at-attention (P21). *[She bends forward, leaning her arms on her thighs.]* I am almost ready to jump (P22).

Supervisor: *[Pacing again.]*... almost ready to jump, how do you feel in your thighs?

Client: Totally tense (P23); somehow, I am standing beside myself (P24).

Supervisor: Where beside you, on your right or left side?

Client: It is funny, somehow on the right side (P25). And I observe myself from outside. ... Yes, and I see how I roll my toes inside.

Supervisor: So, you see it, and how does it feel?

Client: Somehow, I am outside myself; I see it, but I don`t feel it.

Supervisor: Okay. There is one part standing beside another part of you and seeing the other part rolling the toes inside and this outsider is not able to feel the toes...

Client: *[Nods and suddenly says smiling,]* **That's why I stand beside myself.**

Supervisor: **Exactly, and still you are both parts: one observer, who is standing on the right side; and a subject of observation, who is sitting there, is rolling the toes inside. In the situation with your patient, you were the observing outsider. While you are remembering the situation today, it might be possible to associate a little bit with the insider, who is sitting there, rolling the toes inside. What does it feel like?**

Client: *[Sitting with tense thighs, leaning forward and rolling her toes.]* **The toes are rolled inside and cramped (P26) and the feet are icy-cold (P27). My whole back and my neck are stiff (P28).** *[For a short moment, she is sitting there, in a stand-of-attention pose—almost ready to jump. Then she is shaking.]* **Brrr.**

Supervisor: **Brrr...?** *[Shaking also.]*

Client: **I shake it off; I want to get rid of it.**

Supervisor: **How is it now?**

Client: *[Moving her back and neck,]* **Elastic and mobile, composed.** *[Smiling,]* **I am composed again.**

[Having reached the turning point of the UATP, she starts the green list with: mobile, flexible, composed (A28). These words are written on the flipchart by the supervisor.

To stand beside oneself is dissociation from feeling oneself. When the client started to feel herself again, she started an association process and fulfilled it with those little shakings and shiverings, which are well-known reactions from animals as they come out of thanatosis. The supervisor and the client could start now to move upwards on the green side. But the supervisor takes a break.]

Supervisor: *[Repeats all the labels on the red list and asks,]* **Is there anything on the red side we haven't mentioned yet?**

Client: **No, isn't that enough? Most of them I even didn't notice when it happened.**

Supervisor: **How does it feel, what you were only able to observe standing beside yourself?**

Client: **It's strange. As I was standing beside me, I was judging myself. When I associate I have compassion. I become friendlier to myself.** *[She looks thoughtfully and the supervisor waits until she catches the client's gaze again.]*

Supervisor: **Now that you have become your friendly companion... compassion is composing. ...** *[Both are smiling.]* **Let's go forward and explore how it is to be composed again.**

> *[From now on the supervisor will use the salutogenic idiolect of the client in a repetitive manner. Pacing to match the breath of the client, the rate of speech will slow.]*

Imagine yourself in the same situation with your patient... but now being composed again... with a flexible neck and a mobile back. ... If your feet were mobile, what would there be instead of the freezing icy-coldness?

Client: **I would feel them distinctively and warm (A27).** *[She changes the position of her feet. The foot tips point outwards; and while she was talking, she pressed the soles of the feet.]*

Supervisor: **And if your feet were distinctively warm and flexible... what would there be instead of cramps and rolled toes?**

Client: **They are grounded, a contact firm and soft at the same time (A26).** *[Again, she moves her feet a little bit and smiles.]*

Supervisor: Soft and firm contact, the back and the neck warm and flexible, being composed again. ... What would there be, instead of standing beside yourself and observing yourself?

Client: Being one and grounded; I am centered (A25) and see the other person (A24).

Supervisor: If you are mobile... softly and firmly centered and grounded, what will happen to your thighs?

Client: They release, they become soft and relaxed. They are down to earth again (A23).

[This is happening now as she describes it. A change in the shape of her thighs, from oval and high to broad and flat, can be observed beneath the fabric of her trousers. Spontaneously, she has also changed her posture and is leaning backwards.]

Supervisor: What a relief to come down to earth. You are not jumping anymore. Have you noticed how your stand-at-attention has changed?

Client: Yes, I am reclined now; I am looking from inside out (A22). I wait and see, guarded, simply observing. I can patiently wait to see what is coming next (A21).

Supervisor: Grounded and reclined... simply waiting, what's coming next... warm ... soft and firm, what is there instead of tight movements?

Client: Moving is easy and connected. I am congruent (A20).

Supervisor: What is a congruent heartbeat?

Client: [Puts her hand over her the heart.] Peaceful, smooth, and calm (A19).

Supervisor: [Also puts her own hand on the heart and then moves it to the throat.] Reclined and at ease with a calm heart...

grounded soft and firm... what will happen instead of a thick voice?

Client: Then the voice is authentic and certain. I am sure of what I am saying (A18). *[Her voice has already become more grounded, but now she emphasizes the words with resonance.]*

Supervisor: Wow, did you hear the difference in the resonance? How your body tonus and your vocal tone reflect each other?

Client: Yes, I feel and hear it.

Supervisor: When you are authentic and certainly sure of what you are saying... firmly composed and softly released... how does this transform the high and artificial voice?

Client: Although my voice is firm, it is also calm and soft. And as I have compassion with myself, I have empathy with my patient (A17).

Supervisor: Soft and firm as your contact to the ground?

Client: Yes, whole and composed.

Supervisor: Flexible composed and firmly mobile... tonus and tone being one, whole... how does your throat feel?

Client: Humid (A16). *[She swallows.]*

Supervisor: If you only swallow when you are sure... at ease with what is coming up... reclined and centered, seeing the other person... waiting until you are certain to speak with an authentic voice, how will be your belly?

Client: There is a round feeling, comfortably calm and smooth (A15).

Supervisor: Comfort in the belly... mobility in the whole body... an authentic certain voice... when breathing gets easy, what is the difference to staccato and flatness?

Client: It has a deep and soft and steady rhythm, down to my smooth belly (A14). *[Her breathing is already like this.]*

Supervisor: Like now?

Client: *[She takes a deep breath and smiles.]* Yes, like now.

Supervisor: Breathing like this, soft and deep... a calm belly... round... being one in movement and heart... in tonus and tone... comfortably tuned... easy... what is the temperature of your body?

Client: Well, it is comfortably warm (A13). *[She spontaneously takes the next step.]* As well as my hands, which are comfortably warm and dry (A12).

Supervisor: Imagine yourself being grounded in this warm reclined comfort... able to handle the situation flexible and firm, what is there instead of agitation?

Client: I am centered and concentrated on what is happening. My activation is appropriate (A 11).

Supervisor: And what is there instead of tension?

Client: Some tension is fine. It is a balance between stability and flexibility... appropriate (A10). *[She holds her hands like scale pans and moves her body softly from one side to the other.]*

Supervisor: *[Pacing the movement.]* And this soft appropriate balancing... what is there instead of trembling?

Client: *[She brings the hands together and opens them like a funnel in front of her heart.]* If I don't tremble anymore, I am open and calm (A9).

Supervisor: Open and calm... balanced... open view and open heart... standing flexible and firm... even reclined and at ease... composed, what is there instead of obstruction?

Client: I am engaged in what is coming (A8).

Supervisor: Engaged in what is coming up... seeing the other person... waiting and seeing guarded... authentic with an open view... being in a soft rhythm of heartbeat and breath... distinctive feeling of the own body... what is there instead of blockade?

Client: I am confident and capable (A7).

Supervisor: Confidently engaged... capable to balance breath and voice, belly and heart, softness and firmness... centered and being one... waiting and seeing guarded... appropriate activated... composed... how is your forehead?

Client: It is open and upright [Smiling.] and I am upright too, because I give me the right to be up the way I am. That is a very good agreeable feeling (A6).

Supervisor: This very good feeling in your forehead, when you agree the way you are... giving you the right to be... up... and balanced, how does it affect the back of the head?

Client: It is harmonious and relaxed. Reclining not only relaxes my back and my neck, but also my head (A5). My head is a harmonious part of my body now.

Supervisor: Having a balanced harmony in your body and your head... a firm and empathic voice to speak to another person... what happens to this inner warning voice, when you agree with the way, you are?

Client: There is silence and fullness at the same time. I know I have it all (A4).

Supervisor: When you know in your head, your heart and in your belly: You are composed in the right way... capable to engage in what is coming... grounded soft and firm... centered... being one... waiting and seeing guarded... distinctively feeling... once there was a thread running through your everyday life. What will be with this thread?

Client: I can leave it with the patient (A3).

[Although the client hasn't said anything about the conflict with her patient, the supervisor decides to deepen the trance and transfer the beneficial state into the specific problematic situation. For the resource transfer she does not need a formal induction, a simple "...please allow yourself to close your eyes... and imagine yourself in your office..." will be enough. Why is it so easy? The UATP is a conversation, which constantly uses hypnotic elements like pacing, reiteration, slowing down, and leading by a question, suggesting a change. The three parameters, which constitute a trance (state, focus, and suggestion) are built into the protocol. It is a conversational trance and it induces a natural flow, which is open to all kinds of hypnotic strategies; in this case, resource transfer.]

Supervisor: When you know you have everything... to leave it with the patient... being empathic and calm... certain and sure... please allow yourself to close your eyes... just to feel how your body is right now... your muscles... your breath... your heart... your throat... just feel it as it is right now... ease... as it is... it is good enough... to agree... and imagine yourself in your office... sitting reclined and released... waiting and seeing guarded... being there with this special patient... whose health record is in front of you... on the table right now. Observe him... centered and concentrated on what is happening... staying comfortably warm. ... What happened to the cloud?

Client: *[She starts laughing.]* Now the cloud is floating above the patient... and actually it is pretty small (A2).

Supervisor: When you see this small cloud... what do you know about your work as a therapist?

Client: I know, it is his cloud, he has to solve it. He is not the cloud... I can see him... and the cloud. I am capable of helping him, when I am upright and authentic.

Supervisor: In the past, when you met this patient, you had the feeling that something jumped at you. What happened with this?

Client: That is very interesting, now I have a protective cover and I feel secure. My own feelings secure me (A1).

Supervisor: That is very interesting... now you have a protective cover... you are secure. ... What is the color of the protective cover?

Client: It is grey, grey as the cloud was. *[She re-orientates herself and opens her eyes.]* That is weird. What I thought to be a cloud were my own feelings. My feelings clouded my view, because I didn't want to feel what I was feeling. I dissociated from feeling.

Supervisor: You dissociated from feeling, starting to look at yourself from the right side. And now those clouded feelings have become your protective cover. In the very beginning of our meeting, you said that you wanted to understand. What do you understand?

Client: To look after me first is even right, if I do it in a friendly compassionate way. It is a ranking: First to be in harmony with myself, secondly with the patient. *[She looks thoughtful, pauses, then smiles.]* It is not that I haven`t heard it before.

Supervisor: Yes, you have heard it before; what is the difference having gone through this process?

Client: Now it is such a deep experience, it is real understanding. When I heard it, it was logical. But I was not aware what was happening to me. Only through this process of awareness do I understand how I dissociated. *[She laughs.]* It is insight from inside. In experiencing the problem, I found the solution. The key is to stay associated even with disagreeable feelings, compassion. Not to demand strength, but to be soft... empathy starting with myself. What a release.

ABOUT THE EDITOR

Mark P. Jensen, PhD, is a professor and the vice chair for research at the Department of Rehabilitation Medicine, University of Washington, in Seattle, Washington, USA. He has been studying chronic pain and helping individuals effectively manage pain for over 30 years. He has been funded by the National Institutes of Health and other funding agencies to study the efficacy and mechanisms of different treatments for chronic pain, including hypnosis. He has published extensively (seven books and over 500 articles and book chapters) on the topics of pain assessment and treatment.

He has received numerous awards for his writing and scientific contributions including: the Jay Haley Early Career Award for Innovative Contributions to Hypnosis from the International Society of Hypnosis, the Clark L. Hull Award for Scientific Excellence in Writing on Experimental Hypnosis from the *American Journal of Clinical Hypnosis*, the Wilbert E. Fordyce Clinical Investigator Award from the American Pain Society, and both the Distinguished Contributions to Scientific Hypnosis and Distinguished Contributions Professional Hypnosis Awards from the American Psychological Association Division 30, among others.

His book on the use of hypnosis for chronic pain management (*Hypnosis for Chronic Pain Management: Therapist Guide*, published by Oxford University Press) won the 2011 Society for Clinical and Experimental Hypnosis Arthur Shapiro Award: Best Book on Hypnosis. He is also a popular international speaker and workshop facilitator.